This book belongs to:

_____

Copyright © 2019 by Martin Winslow

All rights reserved.

No part of this book may be reproduced in any form or by any electronic or mechanical means, including information storage and retrieval systems, without written permission from the author, except for the use of brief quotations in a book review.

Layout and design by Sarah Benz.

New Testament 260

 A 260 day New Testament reading plan and navigation tool

"Be diligent to present yourself approved to God as a workman who does not need to be ashamed, accurately handling the word of truth."

2 Timothy 2:15

MARTIN WINSLOW

For my "Arrows"

Noah, Anna, Emma, Laura, and Nati

"Behold, children are a gift of the Lord,

The fruit of the womb is a reward.

Like arrows in the hand of a warrior,

So are the children of one's youth.

How blessed is the man whose quiver is full of them;

They will not be ashamed

When they speak with their enemies in the gate."

Psalm 127:3-5

Table of Contents

[Navigate your way through the New Testament]

6-7 Preface

8-13 Gospel of Matthew

13-16 Gospel of Mark

16-21 Gospel of Luke

21-25 Gospel of John

25-31 Book of Acts

31-33 Book of Romans

36 Book of Romans

36-42 Books of I & II Corinthians

42-43 Book of Galatians

43-44 Book of Ephesians

44-45 Book of Philippians

45-46 Book of Colossians

46-47 Books of I & II Thessalonians

48-49 Books of I & II Timothy

50 Book of Titus

50 Book of Philemon

50-53 Book of Hebrews

53-54 Book of James

54-55 Books of I & II Peter

56-57 Books of I, II & III John

57 Book of Jude

57-61 Book of Revelation

Preface

Most people don't realize that the 52 weeks of our solar year excluding weekends leaves exactly 260 days. That is 260 days of Mondays through Fridays. Fewer people probably realize that there are also exactly 260 chapters in the New Testament. Do you see where I am heading? If one chapter a day is read out of the New Testament for five days a week, the New Testament can be read in exactly one year!

This reading program exists to help children and adults become faithful readers of the New Testament. It also helps the user to remember an important truth out of every chapter of the New Testament along the way. Each important truth of the day is called a "paraphrase" of the chapter and should be memorized. After these truths have been memorized, they help a child or adult navigate the New Testament quickly. If you would like to learn the New Testament paraphrases through songs, this option will be available for each N.T. book on the website **www.nextgenerationfaithfulness.com**. Each song can be individually purchased and downloaded separately. The daily paraphrases are set to music for each New Testament book. This allows children the ability to learn these paraphrases very quickly. After each day's reading mark the box and practice saying the paraphrase a few times. Each morning take a couple of minutes to review the paraphrases before going to the next chapter's reading. I originally created this program for students at the christian school where I was headmaster. Many students through the years were capable of memorizing all 260 paraphrases! Another great setting to use this is in a family worship setting each day at home.

For hundreds of years many evangelical denominations have taught creeds and catechism to their children. These tools have been very helpful for laying a theological foundation in the lives of young people. I personally know the value of catechism because my wife and I catechize our children. **What is a catechism?** It is basically questions and answers memorized about the Christian faith. Catechism comes from the Greek word *"katakeo"* and means *"I instruct."* The catechism has a questioner and an answerer. There are several catechisms for families to choose from if they are interested in instructing their children about the basic doctrines of the faith. Almost all catechisms are theological in nature. In other words, the questions being asked to the child have their answers based upon a holistic understanding of scripture. While traditional catechism is great about answering worldview issues, it lacks in equipping young people the ability to locate where the truth memorized is found in the Bible. A typical catechism may start young children out as follows:

A typical catechism may start young children out as follows:

Question: Who made you?

Answer: God made me.

Question: What else did God make?

Answer: God made all things.

New Testament 260 gives the knowledge of where specific truth is taught in the New Testament. As children get older they will always know "God makes the rules about marriage" is found in I Corinthians 7. This will allow them to know exactly where they should be looking for spiritual truth regarding relationships. They memorize both the truth and where it is located in the Bible by using this important tool. I Peter 3 says, *"But sanctify Christ as Lord in your hearts, always being ready to make a defense to everyone who asks you to give an account for the hope that is in you, yet with gentleness and reverence." (I Peter 3:15)*

Memorizing the chapters and paraphrases will put key verses and themes into the mind, stored up like a treasure house of wisdom to draw upon when needed. Learning **New Testament 260** could help anyone defend the doctrine of the divinity of Christ or the trinity (John 1 "Jesus is God," Acts 5 "The Holy Spirit is God.") These paraphrases truly help build a solid biblical foundation. They are also very helpful for knowing key stories in the New Testament like Jesus feeding 4,000 *(Matt. 15)* or Jesus teaching about the greatest commandment *(Matt. 22)*. **New Testament 260** will allow immediate knowledge of where Paul's first, second, and third missionary journeys were *(Acts 13, 15, 18)*. This is a priceless tool for those who wish to navigate through their scriptures with fluidity. Simply mark the bubble next to each paraphrase after reading and memorizing each day. Marking the bubble in will ensure that the reader will not lose their place. If reading through the New Testament in exactly one year is not important to you, you can still utilize this tool at your own pace.

Important directions before starting:

It would be perfect if every 1st of January started on a Monday. However, this is not to be. In order for this reading plan to work out well the readings may have to be doubled up for the first couple of days so that you start week 2 out on "day 6."

For example, let's say that the 1st of January is a Tuesday. Simply read Matthew 1 and 2 on Tuesday and memorize the paraphrases for those two days. Then by day 3 the reading program is on target. Or, let's pretend that January 1st is on a Wednesday. Simply read Matthew 1-2 on Wednesday and 3-4 on Thursday and memorize the 4 paraphrases. Then on day 5, the reading program is right on target! It may sound like a lot to memorize, but DON'T WORRY! The songs make the memorization very easy. Repeat the paraphrases several times each day in order. Enjoy this tool and may God bless your reading of the entire New Testament!

All scriptures taken from the NASB Bible.

The Gospel of Matthew Matthew 1-5

Week 1

Weekly reading overview:

This weekly reading will introduce the person and teachings of Jesus Christ. Matthew 1 begins with the genealogy of Jesus. The genealogy connects Jesus to Abraham in the Old Testament, Jesus is the promised Messiah! Matthew 2 demonstrates that Jesus is a Messiah who saves men from every nation of the world. He is not only a Messiah for Jews but the Magi from the East as well (Gentile nations). In Chapter 3, we meet John the Baptist. John preaches in the wilderness and baptizes Jesus. In Chapter 4, Jesus endures being tempted by the devil. He never gives in to the lies of the devil but trusts God! Chapter 5 begins with the most famous sermon ever preached, The Sermon on the Mount.

The Gospel of Matthew	Week 1 Chapter paraphrase verses to memorize
☐ Day 1: Matthew 1	Jesus is born of a virgin
☐ Day 2: Matthew 2	The wise men worship Jesus
☐ Day 3: Matthew 3	John preaches in the wilderness and Jesus is baptized
☐ Day 4: Matthew 4	Jesus is tempted by the devil
☐ Day 5: Matthew 5	Jesus came to fulfill the law and the prophets

Review these each day and listen to the songs!

 Key verse:

"Do not think that I came to abolish the Law or the Prophets; I did not come to abolish but to fulfill."
Matthew 5:17

 **Did you know?**

Matthew (Mt. 9:9) is the same person as Levi (Mk. 2:14). Matthew was his Greek name and Levi was his Hebrew name.

 **Prayer for the week:**

Dear Father, help me to resist temptations when they come my way like Jesus did. Help me to know the scriptures well enough so that I can quote them when I am in difficult situations.

The Gospel of Matthew

Matthew 6-10

Week 2

Weekly reading overview:

In Chapters 6 and 7, Jesus continues to preach The Sermon on the Mount. The lessons that He teaches here are very rich in meaning. One very important thing that Jesus does in this sermon is to teach His disciples the Lord's prayer. This prayer is very popular. Have you memorized it? If not, take the time to do that this week along with memorizing the paraphrases! After this great sermon, Jesus begins healing many people of their sicknesses and infirmities and also sends out the 12 disciples to heal and minister to the needs of the people. He warns them this will not be easy, and they should expect persecution.

The Gospel of Matthew	Week 2 Chapter paraphrase verses to memorize
☐ Day 6: Matthew 6	Jesus teaches his disciples the Lord's prayer
☐ Day 7: Matthew 7	Jesus warns about false prophets
☐ Day 8: Matthew 8	Jesus cleanses the leper
☐ Day 9: Matthew 9	Jesus heals many and calls Matthew
☐ Day 10: Matthew 10	Jesus sends out the 12 disciples

Review these each day and listen to the songs!

Key verse:

"Pray, then, in this way: Our Father who is in heaven, Hallowed be Your name. Your kingdom come. Your will be done, on earth as it is in heaven. Give us this day our daily bread and forgive us our debts, as we also have forgiven our debtors. And do not lead us into temptation but deliver us from evil. For Yours is the kingdom and the power and the glory forever. Amen."
Matthew 6:9-13

Did you know?

Matthew, Mark, Luke and John are all called Gospels. They are called that because each of them tell us the story of the life of Jesus. Do you know which Gospel has the most chapters in it?...Matthew! It has 28.

Prayer for the week:

Dear Father, help me to be a person of prayer. Help me to memorize the model prayer that You gave to Your disciples so that I might remember the things that I should pray.

The Gospel of Matthew

Matthew 11-15

Week 3

Weekly reading overview:

As Jesus continues His ministry in the Gospel of Matthew, He preaches in many cities. Unfortunately, many people did not turn from their sins. Jesus warns that a day of judgment is coming for them. Jesus and His disciples are accused by a group of people called the "Pharisees" of doing work on the Sabbath day, which is supposed to be a day of rest. Jesus reminds the Pharisees that He is the Creator and Lord of the Sabbath day. Jesus' disciples were hungry and the Pharisees should have had compassion on them, but they didn't. In Chapter 13, Jesus teaches that when someone discovers His Kingdom, he is willing to leave everything behind to know Him! John 14 tells us the story of John's death. In Chapter 15, Jesus does an incredible miracle by feeding 4,000 people at one time!

The Gospel of Matthew	Week 3 Chapter paraphrase verses to memorize
☐ Day 11: Matthew 11	Jesus warns the unrepenting cities
☐ Day 12: Matthew 12	Jesus is Lord of the Sabbath
☐ Day 13: Matthew 13	Jesus teaches about the Kingdom of God
☐ Day 14: Matthew 14	John the Baptist is beheaded
☐ Day 15: Matthew 15	Jesus feeds 4,000

Review these each day and listen to the songs!

Key verse:

"The kingdom of heaven is like a treasure hidden in the field, which a man found and hid again; and from joy over it he goes and sells all that he has and buys that field."
Matthew 13:44

Did you know?

Matthew Ch. 14 mentions Jesus doing a miracle where 5,000 men were fed along with women and children as well. In Ch. 15, Jesus again feeds the multitudes. This time 4,000 men along with women and children. Even though it seems as though more people were at the first feeding than the second, more food was actually left over after the larger feeding in Ch. 14. 12 full baskets were left in Ch. 14:20, while seven large baskets were left over in 15:38, assuming of course the baskets were the same size.

Prayer for the week:

Dear Father, thank You for the testimony of men like John the Baptist. I thank You Lord that he was faithful to You even until the end of his life. Help me to be faithful to You today.

The Gospel of Matthew

Matthew 16-20

Week 4

Weekly reading overview:

You will love this week's readings! In Chapter 16, Jesus asks his disciples "who do people say that the Son of Man is?" This is a question that every single person in the world must answer. Who do you say that Jesus is? The transfiguration of Jesus is an event where Jesus shows His glory to Peter, James, and John. Jesus teaches His disciples about personal conflict and how to handle it, followed by the importance of forgiveness. In Chapter 19, Jesus talks about the importance of marriage commitment and challenges a wealthy man. Chapter 20 tells us of Jesus' encounter with two men who are blind. They believe that He is God's Messiah and call Him the "Son of David." Jesus heals them!

The Gospel of Matthew	Week 4 Chapter paraphrase verses to memorize
☐ Day 16: Matthew 16	Peter confesses Jesus is the Christ
☐ Day 17: Matthew 17	The transfiguration of Jesus
☐ Day 18: Matthew 18	Jesus teaches about discipline and forgiveness
☐ Day 19: Matthew 19	Jesus teaches about divorce and talks to the rich young ruler
☐ Day 20: Matthew 20	Jesus heals two blind men

Review these each day and listen to the songs!

 Key verse:

"Now when Jesus came into the district of Caesarea Philippi, He was asking His disciples, 'Who do people say that the Son of Man is?' And they said, 'Some say John the Baptist; and others, Elijah; but still others, Jeremiah, or one of the prophets.' He said to them, 'But who do you say that I am?' Simon Peter answered, 'You are the Christ, the Son of the living God.'"
Matthew 16:13-16

 Did you know?

When Peter confesses that Jesus is the "Christ," he is saying that Jesus is the King. Christ is a Greek word that means "anointed one." Kings are usually anointed by prophets in the Old Testament as David was anointed by Samuel in I Samuel 16:13. Jesus is the forever King prophesied about in the Old Testament who is the son of David (II Samuel 7:12-17).

 Prayer for the week:

Dear Father, thank You for the testimony of Peter. I know that Jesus is the Son of God. Help me today to not be ashamed of this truth and to tell others about Your love.

The Gospel of Matthew

Matthew 21-25

Week 5

Weekly reading overview:

Jesus continues to tell parables in the Gospel of Matthew to illustrate important truths for the people. In Chapter 22, Jesus is challenged to come up with an answer to a very difficult question. What is the greatest commandment? In Chapter 23, Jesus reminds the religious leaders that just because they look religious, doesn't mean they actually are. Hypocrites are people who tell others not to do things that they themselves are guilty of doing. As the disciples admire the beauty of the temple in Jerusalem, Jesus predicts a day when the temple will be completely destroyed. Interestingly enough, this comes true 40 years later when the Romans destroyed it! In Chapter 25, Jesus tells three parables that remind Christians to be ready for His coming.

The Gospel of Matthew	Week 5 Chapter paraphrase verses to memorize
☐ Day 21: Matthew 21	Jesus tells the parables of the two sons and the parable of the landowner
☐ Day 22: Matthew 22	Jesus teaches about the greatest commandment
☐ Day 23: Matthew 23	Jesus warns about hypocrisy
☐ Day 24: Matthew 24	Jesus predicts the destruction of the temple
☐ Day 25: Matthew 25	Jesus tells the parable of the ten virgins, the talents and the sheep and the goats

Review these each day and listen to the songs!

 Key verse:

 **Did you know?**

 **Prayer for the week:**

"But when the Pharisees heard that Jesus had silenced the Sadducees, they gathered themselves together. One of them, a lawyer, asked Him a question, testing Him, 'Teacher, which is the great commandment in the Law?' And He said to him, **'You shall love the Lord your God with all your heart, and with all your soul, and with all your mind.'** This is the great and foremost commandment. The second is like it, **'You shall love your neighbor as yourself.'** On these two commandments depend the whole Law and the Prophets."
Matthew 22:34-40

A parable is a short story that Jesus tells to illustrate a truth. We see many of these short stories told in the Gospel of Matthew. Each story is told to help the people listening to Jesus understand an important spiritual truth in everyday language. While the parable itself may have never happened, we know that similar things do often occur in everyday life.

Dear Father, help me to love You more than anything and to love my neighbor as myself. In order to do this, I pray that You help me to not be selfish and to put the needs of others above my own.

The Gospels of Matthew / Mark

Matthew 26-28 + Mark 1-2

Week 6

Weekly reading overview:

Matthew 26 begins Jesus' journey to the cross. While Jesus was at the house of Simon the leper, a woman comes and pours perfume on His head to prepare Him for His burial. Before the Chapter ends, Judas betrays Jesus, and He is arrested in the Garden of Gethsemane. Chapter 27 details His horrible journey to the cross, His beating and crucifixion for our sins. In Chapter 28 after 3 days in the grave, Jesus is raised from the dead just like He predicted! He tells His disciples that they are to go and tell the Gospel to all of the nations! This week we also begin in the Gospel of Mark. Matthew starts with a genealogy of Jesus and His birth, but Mark begins with Jesus' public ministry when Jesus is in His 30s. Jesus begins after His temptation by preaching in Capernaum, Peter's hometown. In Mark 2, Jesus dramatically heals a paralyzed man.

The Gospels of Matthew / Mark	Week 6 Chapter paraphrase verses to memorize
☐ Day 26: Matthew 26	Jesus is anointed for his burial
☐ Day 27: Matthew 27	Jesus is mocked and crucified
☐ Day 28: Matthew 28	Jesus gives the Great Commission to His disciples
☐ Day 29: Mark 1	Jesus preaches and heals in Capernaum
☐ Day 30: Mark 2	Jesus heals the paralytic and teaches about the Sabbath

*Review these each day and listen to the songs!

 Key verse:

"And Jesus came up and spoke to them, saying, 'All authority has been given to Me in heaven and on earth. Go therefore and make disciples of all the nations, baptizing them in the name of the Father and the Son and the Holy Spirit, teaching them to observe all that I commanded you; and lo, I am with you always, even to the end of the age.'"
Matthew 28:18-20

 Did you know?

Matthew and Luke are the two Gospels that mention the virgin birth. Mark begins at the beginning of Jesus' public ministry when he is around 30 years old. The Gospel of John begins in the beginning.

 **Prayer for the week:**

Dear Father, I thank You for the sacrifice of Jesus in my place. Thank You that He went through the suffering that I deserved. Help me to never take His death in my place for granted. I also thank You for raising Him from the dead.

The Gospel of Mark

Mark 3-7

 Week 7

Weekly reading overview:

This week Jesus chooses His 12 disciples, and they are named in Mark 3. He teaches the parable of the sower in Chapter 4 followed by an incredible miracle of raising a little girl from the dead in Chapter 5. Jesus heals a man filled with multiple demons in Chapter 6. The demons are sent into nearby pigs and plunge off the side of a cliff killing the pigs. In Chapter 7, Jesus confronts the Pharisees and exposes their hypocrisy. Many of the Pharisees were giving their money to the temple instead of helping their own parents who were in need. Jesus tells them that they are not honoring their parents!

The Gospel of Mark	Week 7 Chapter paraphrase verses to memorize
☐ Day 31: Mark 3	Jesus chooses the 12 disciples
☐ Day 32: Mark 4	Jesus teaches the parable of the sower
☐ Day 33: Mark 5	Jesus raises a girl from the dead
☐ Day 34: Mark 6	Jesus heals in Genessaret
☐ Day 35: Mark 7	Don't let tradition invalidate the Word of God

*Review these each day and listen to the songs!

 **Key verse:**

 **Did you know?**

 **Prayer for the week:**

"Taking the child by the hand, He said to her, 'Talitha kum!' (which translated means, 'Little girl, I say to you, get up!'). Immediately the girl got up and began to walk, for she was twelve years old. And immediately they were completely astounded."
Mark 5:41-42

The difference between Jesus raising this girl from the dead and His resurrection is significant. This little girl was brought back to life and later died again. Jesus was raised never to die again!

Lord, I pray that this week my life will be like the good ground that receives the seed of Your Word. Help me to love and serve You like I should. In Jesus' name, Amen.

The Gospel of Mark

Mark 8-12

Week 8

Weekly reading overview:

This week you will see Jesus predict His suffering, death, and resurrection three times in a section called "The Heart of Mark's Gospel." Jesus reminds His disciples that the key to being honored is by being the servant. Chapter 10 is the famous story of Jesus healing blind Bartimaeus. In Mark Chapter 11, Jesus runs the money changers out of the Temple, because they are robbing people of their money. Jesus rebukes them and reminds them that God's Temple is to be a place of prayer, not people stealing from others. In Chapter 12 Jesus teaches us about a widow who gave all of the money she had to God. Jesus tells us that her offering was worth more than all of those who gave larger amounts because they gave out of their abundance. The widow gave from her poverty.

The Gospel of Mark	Week 8 Chapter paraphrase verses to memorize
☐ Day 36: Mark 8	Jesus predicts His death and resurrection
☐ Day 37: Mark 9	If anyone wants to be first, he shall be last of all and servant of all
☐ Day 38: Mark 10	Jesus heals blind Bartimaeus
☐ Day 39: Mark 11	Jesus cleanses the Temple
☐ Day 40: Mark 12	Jesus teaches about the widow's mite

Review these each day and listen to the songs!

Key verse:

"For He was teaching His disciples and telling them, The Son of Man is to be delivered into the hands of men, and they will kill Him; and when He has been killed, He will rise three days later."
Mark 9:31

Did you know?

Isaiah prophesied that when the Messiah came, He would be able to open the eyes of the blind. Healing the blind is something that we see only Jesus do in the Bible (Isaiah 35:1-5; 42:6,7).

Prayer for the week:

Lord, this week I pray that I will give generously of all that I have like the poor widow who gave her mite. Thank You for blessing me with so much. Help me to bless others with what I have.

The Gospels of Mark / Luke

Mark 13-16 + Luke 1

Week 9

Weekly reading overview:

After Jesus predicts His death and resurrection three times in Mark, he tells the disciples that He will return again to them. He tells them that God will judge Jerusalem and eventually gather together all Christians. After Jesus is arrested, the disciples begin to scatter. Peter becomes afraid and denies Christ three times. After Jesus appears before Pilate, He is eventually turned over to the Jews to be crucified for our sins. Chapter 16 tells us, as do all the Gospels, that on Sunday, there was an empty tomb. Christ has been raised! This week you will also begin the Gospel of Luke. John the Baptist comes before Jesus and is called the "forerunner." John prepares the hearts of the people to receive Jesus as the Messiah.

The Gospels of Mark / Luke	Week 9 Chapter paraphrase verses to memorize
☐ Day 41: Mark 13	Jesus promises that He is coming again
☐ Day 42: Mark 14	Peter denies Jesus three times
☐ Day 43: Mark 15	Jesus is killed and buried
☐ Day 44: Mark 16	Jesus is raised from the dead
☐ Day 45: Luke 1	The forerunner is born!

Review these each day and listen to the songs!

 Key verse:

 **Did you know?**

 **Prayer for the week:**

"Looking up, they saw that the stone had been rolled away, although it was extremely large. Entering the tomb, they saw a young man sitting at the right, wearing a white robe; and they were amazed. And he said to them, 'Do not be amazed; you are looking for Jesus the Nazarene, who has been crucified. He has risen; He is not here; behold, here is the place where they laid Him.'"
Mark 16:4-6

The Bible prophesied that before the coming of the Messiah (Jesus), Elijah would appear to the nation of Israel (Malachi 4:5-6). Jesus said that John the Baptist was the Elijah who was to come before Him (Matthew 11:14). Luke 1:17 said that John the Baptist came in the spirit and power of Elijah.

Dear Heavenly Father, I thank You for raising Jesus from the dead. Thank You that He conquered sin and death for all Christians. Help me today to trust in Your resurrection power in my life.

The Gospel of Luke | Luke 2-6

 # Week 10

Weekly reading overview:

Luke 2 tells us about the faith of two very interesting people, Simeon and Anna. God told Simeon that he would not die until he had seen the Messiah with his own eyes. This prophecy came true in Luke 2! Anna, a very devout widow, prayed day and night for God to send His Messiah and also lives to see the baby Jesus at age 84! Luke goes on to introduce John the Baptist who tells the Pharisees that if they have truly repented, their lives should begin to look different. He tells them true repentance from sin leads to fruit in a person's life. In Chapter 3 Luke tells us about Jesus beginning His ministry and naming the twelve disciples. He also encourages His disciples to build their house upon the rock of His words.

The Gospel of Luke	Week 10 Chapter paraphrase verses to memorize
☐ Day 46: Luke 2	Simeon and Anna see the Messiah
☐ Day 47: Luke 3	John says to bear fruit in keeping with repentance
☐ Day 48: Luke 4	Jesus begins his public ministry
☐ Day 49: Luke 5	Jesus calls James, John, Peter, and Matthew
☐ Day 50: Luke 6	Jesus says to build your house on the rock

Review these each day and listen to the songs!

Key verse:

"Everyone who comes to Me and hears My words and acts on them, I will show you whom he is like: he is like a man building a house, who dug deep and laid a foundation on the rock; and when a flood occurred, the torrent burst against that house and could not shake it, because it had been well built."
Luke 6:47-48

Did you know?

Joseph and Mary lost the Son of God (Jesus) in Jerusalem for 3 days (Luke 2:46). Can you imagine what their prayers must have been like those three days? "Dear God, we need help. We lost your son......."

Prayer for the week:

Dear Lord, please help me this week to listen, learn, and love Your Word. Help me to obey Your Words and be like the man who built his house upon the rock. Thank You for loving me! In Jesus' name, Amen.

The Gospel of Luke   Luke 7-11

Week 11

Weekly reading overview:

This week is some great reading. Jesus heals the Centurion's servant. A Centurion was a Roman army officer in charge of 80 men. Jesus shows His power over the demons in Chapter 8. In Chapter 9 Jesus tells His disciples that to follow Him means being willing to give your life for Him. In Chapter 10 one of Jesus' most famous parables tells the story of a kind Samaritan helping a man who was robbed. In Luke 11 Jesus argues with the religious leaders, telling them that He has come from heaven and is on a mission from God the Father!

The Gospel of Luke	Week 11 Chapter paraphrase verses to memorize
☐ Day 51: Luke 7	Jesus heals the Centurion's servant
☐ Day 52: Luke 8	Jesus heals the demoniac
☐ Day 53: Luke 9	If anyone wishes to come after me, he must deny himself, take up his cross and follow me
☐ Day 54: Luke 10	Jesus tells the parable of the Good Samaritan
☐ Day 55: Luke 11	A house divided against itself will not stand

Review these each day and listen to the songs!

Key verse:

"If anyone wishes to come after me, he must deny himself, take up his cross and follow me."
Luke 9:23

Did you know?

Samaritans were considered unclean by the Jews in the first century. Jews walked around the city of Samaria to avoid any contact with Samaritans. For Jesus to make a Samaritan the hero of a story would have certainly upset many people.

Prayer for the week:

Dear Father, help me to be willing to pick up my cross and follow Jesus. Help me to not allow anything in this world to come between me and my relationship with You. I pray for You to grow me in my faith in Jesus this week, in Jesus' name, Amen.

The Gospel of Luke

Luke 12-16

Week 12

Weekly reading overview:

Jesus warns in Chapter 12 that following Him will be very difficult at times. It may cost people their friendships. Jesus goes on in Chapter 13 to speak about the Kingdom of God and its growth. It starts off like a tiny seed but grows into a huge tree. This is the same way God works in our life as He matures us in Christ. Luke 14 challenges all believers to be willing to die for following Jesus. In Chapter 15 Jesus shows that He loves sinners and has come to help them have a relationship with God. Chapter 16 is a warning about greed and ignoring neighbors. The rich man in the story who never served God or his fellow man ends up in hell while Lazarus who serves God ends up in paradise. The man in hell asked to come back and warn his brothers about the torment of hell, but God wouldn't allow it.

The Gospel of Luke	Week 12 Chapter paraphrase verses to memorize
☐ Day 56: Luke 12	Living for the truth can cause division
☐ Day 57: Luke 13	Jesus tells the parable of the mustard seed and the leaven
☐ Day 58: Luke 14	Whoever does not carry his own cross and come after me cannot be my disciple
☐ Day 59: Luke 15	Jesus tells the parables of the lost sheep, lost coin, and the prodigal son
☐ Day 60: Luke 16	Jesus tells the parable of the rich man and Lazarus

*Review these each day and listen to the songs!

Key verse:

"I tell you that in the same way, there will be more joy in heaven over one sinner who repents than over ninety-nine righteous persons who need no repentance."
Luke 15:7

Did you know?

The story of the prodigal son is more of a story about the bad attitude of the older brother than it is about the younger brother. Jesus tells the three parables in Luke 15 because the Scribes and Pharisees were grumbling about the kindness that Jesus was showing to sinners (Luke 15:2).

Prayer for the week:

Lord, please help me to treat others who don't know You with the kindness that Jesus showed others. Please use me to show them the light of the Gospel and Your desire to have a relationship with them.

The Gospel of Luke

Luke 17-21

Week 13

Weekly reading overview:

What a great week of Bible reading this week! Jesus cleanses 10 lepers in Chapter 17. Pay attention to what happens next. It is pretty disappointing. Chapter 18 is about staying consistent in prayer with God. Don't give up, but be persistent in your prayers! Chapter 19 is the great story of Zacchaeus climbing the tree to catch Jesus passing by. The greatest part of the story occurs when Zacchaeus repents of his sin and gives back to all the people that he cheated in the past! Jesus teaches the Sadducees in Chapter 20 that a bodily resurrection can happen. In Luke 21 Jesus tells his disciples that one day He will return again.

The Gospel of Luke	Week 13 Chapter paraphrase verses to memorize
☐ Day 61: Luke 17	Jesus cleanses 10 lepers
☐ Day 62: Luke 18	Jesus tells parables on prayer
☐ Day 63: Luke 19	Zacchaeus believes in Jesus
☐ Day 64: Luke 20	Jesus teaches that there is a resurrection
☐ Day 65: Luke 21	Jesus speaks of his return

Review these each day and listen to the songs!

Key verse:

"Zacchaeus stopped and said to the Lord, 'Behold, Lord, half of my possessions I will give to the poor, and if I have defrauded anyone of anything, I will give back four times as much.' And Jesus said to him, 'Today salvation has come to this house, because he, too, is a son of Abraham. For the Son of Man has come to seek and to save that which was lost.'"
Luke 19: 8-10

Did you know?

The Sadducees didn't believe that life carried on beyond the grave. They rejected any idea of an after-life and tried to trick Jesus in their question to Him.

Prayer for the week:

"Jesus, help me to always give You thanks for the things that You do in my life. Help me to never forget to give You praise in my life and thanks in my prayers."

The Gospels of Luke / John

Luke 22-24 + John 1-2

Week 14

Weekly reading overview:

Luke 22 leads us down the road toward Jesus' crucifixion. Jesus tells his disciples to prepare the Passover meal. At the meal he tells them He will be sacrificed like the Passover lamb. In Chapter 23 we read of His horrible death. Of course we should be super grateful that God used this for our good. Simon an Egyptian man from Cyrene helps Jesus carry the cross to the place of His death. In Chapter 24 Jesus appears as the resurrected Lord. Death could not defeat Him. He appears to some men on the road to Emmaus and tells them the scriptures had prophesied about the death, burial, and resurrection of the Messiah. The men realized that they were talking with Jesus. John's gospel is different than Matthew, Mark, and Luke. Matthew and Luke start with the virgin birth of Jesus. Mark starts with Jesus' public ministry, but John goes all the way back to the beginning and shows that Jesus is the Creator. Jesus is God! In Chapter two Jesus does His first public miracle during His ministry at Cana in Galilee.

The Gospels of Luke / John	Week 14 Chapter paraphrase verses to memorize
☐ Day 66: Luke 22	Jesus' disciples prepare the Passover
☐ Day 67: Luke 23	Simon bears the cross of Jesus
☐ Day 68: Luke 24	Jesus appears on the road to Emmaus and ascends to heaven
☐ Day 69: John 1	Jesus is God
☐ Day 70: John 2	Jesus turns the water into wine

*Review these each day and listen to the songs!

 Key verse:

 **Did you know?**

 **Prayer for the week:**

"In the beginning was the Word, and the Word was with God, and the Word was God. He was in the beginning with God."
John 1:1

Christians believe in the trinity. That means there is only one true God who is at the same time three distinct persons known as Father, Son, and Holy Spirit. John 1:3 tells us about Jesus, "All things came into being through Him, and apart from Him nothing came into being that has come into being." Jesus is Creator.

Jesus, I thank You that You are the resurrected Lord of glory! Thank You for not only dying for my sins but raising again from the dead and conquering death for me. Help me to worship You as I should in Jesus' name. Amen.

The Gospel of John

John 3-7

📅 Week 15

Weekly reading overview:

John 3 starts out with the very famous story of Nicodemus. Nicodemus comes to Jesus at night and wants to know more about who He is. Jesus tells him that he must be born again! In John 4 Jesus takes a trip to Samaria. There He meets a woman and tells her that He is the Messiah. Jesus heals a man in John Chapter 5 who had been ill for 38 years! In John 6 Jesus feeds the multitudes by a miraculous work and also appears to the disciples walking on water. In John 7, Jesus tells His hearers that He is the water of life. If anyone drinks from the water He provides, he will never thirst again. This means that anyone who trusts in Jesus for salvation can live with God forever in heaven.

The Gospel of John	Week 15 Chapter paraphrase verses to memorize
☐ Day 71: John 3	Jesus tells Nicodemus the way of life
☐ Day 72: John 4	Jesus tells the woman at the well the way of life
☐ Day 73: John 5	Jesus heals the man at the pool
☐ Day 74: John 6	Jesus feeds 5,000 and walks on water
☐ Day 75: John 7	Jesus is the water of life

Review these each day and listen to the songs!

📖 Key verse:

"For God so loved the world, that He gave His only begotten Son, that whoever believes in Him shall not perish, but have eternal life."
John 3:16

Did you know?

The story of Jesus and the woman at Jacob's well in Samaria is very similar to the story of Jacob meeting Rachel at a nearby well. The story is recorded in Genesis 29.

🙏 Prayer for the week:

Dear Father, I thank You for the story of Nicodemus. Help me to remember that the world needs the Good News of the Gospel. Help me to be like Jesus in telling the world that they must be born again.

The Gospel of John   John 8-12

Week 16

Weekly reading overview:

What an amazing week of reading you are about to have! The first main story shows a woman caught in adultery. The people want to kill her for breaking the 7th commandment *(Ex. 20:14)*. Wait till you see how Jesus handles it! John 9 tells a very cool story of Jesus healing a blind man. The religious leaders are so confused about this miracle that they even interview the blind man's parents. In John 10, Jesus shows Himself to be like a shepherd for His church. We are the sheep of His pasture (we need to keep following our shepherd). An amazing miracle occurs in Chapter 11. Jesus raises his friend Lazarus from the dead after he had been dead several days. In John 12, a woman named Mary anoints Jesus for His burial. Jesus is headed to Jerusalem and toward the cross.

The Gospel of John	Week 16 Chapter paraphrase verses to memorize
☐ Day 76: John 8	Jesus forgives the woman caught in adultery and claims to be God
☐ Day 77: John 9	Jesus heals a blind man
☐ Day 78: John 10	Jesus is the good shepherd
☐ Day 79: John 11	Jesus raises Lazarus from the dead
☐ Day 80: John 12	Mary anoints Jesus and He enters Jerusalem

*Review these each day and listen to the songs!

 **Key verse:**

"Straightening up, Jesus said to her, 'Woman, where are they? Did no one condemn you?' She said, 'No one, Lord.' And Jesus said, 'I do not condemn you, either. Go. From now on sin no more.'"
John 8:10

 **Did you know?**

We have no original writings of Jesus. All of the New Testament is written by His followers. When Jesus stoops to write on the ground in the story of the woman caught in adultery, it is the only record of Him ever writing anything. By the way, scripture never tells us what He wrote in the dirt!

 **Prayer for the week:**

Father, we thank You that You forgive sinners. We thank You for the compassion of Jesus toward the woman caught in adultery. We also ask You to help us remember that forgiveness demands a response from us and You told her to sin no more. Help us to grow toward You and away from sin.

The Gospel of John

John 13-17

Week 17

Weekly reading overview:

John 13 tells the story of Jesus having the last supper. The bread and juice remind us of His body and blood that will be sacrificed for our sins. In John 14, Jesus' disciples become distressed that He is leaving them. He tells them He must go away (die). He also comforts them by promising to prepare a place for them. John 15 encourages each of us to remember that without Jesus we can do nothing. John 16 is one of the most important passages of scripture. Jesus promises that His Holy Spirit will come to the church. In Acts Chapter 2 we will see the fulfillment of this prophecy. In John 17 as the time of Jesus' betrayal is at hand, we see Jesus pray for His disciples to stay unified and strong. He prays for the disciples to stay as "one" as God the Father and God the Son are "One."

The Gospel of John	Week 17 Chapter paraphrase verses to memorize
☐ Day 81: John 13	Jesus has the last supper with His disciples
☐ Day 82: John 14	Jesus comforts His disciples
☐ Day 83: John 15	We should keep Jesus' commands and love one another
☐ Day 84: John 16	Jesus promises the Holy Spirit
☐ Day 85: John 17	Jesus prays for His disciples

Review these each day and listen to the songs!

 **Key verse:**

 **Did you know?**

 **Prayer for the week:**

"A new commandment I give to you, that you love one another, even as I have loved you, that you also love one another. By this all men will know that you are My disciples, if you have love for one another."
John 13:34-45

All the miracles in the gospel of John are called "signs." When Jesus says in John 14 "I am the Way," we can understand that all of the signs Jesus performed were pointing to Him as THE WAY to God. The signs of Jesus are like signs on a road that point you in the direction you need to go. Jesus' signs show Him to be the Way.

Dear Father, help me this week to remember that the world will recognize that I belong to You by my love for other Christians. Help me to love others the way Jesus did.

The Gospel of John / Book of Acts

John 18-21 + Acts 1

Week 18

Weekly reading overview:

Judas, with greed in his heart, betrayed the Son of God. John 18 is a sad story about Judas hardening his heart toward Christ. In John 19 Jesus is crucified for our sin on the cross. When we trust in Jesus' finished work on the cross and give our lives to Him, we become born-again. In John 20, we see Jesus making a believer out of doubting Thomas. He appeared to Thomas to prove that He was Thomas' Lord and God. In John 21 we see Jesus appear to His disciples providing proof that He had conquered death and the grave. This week you also begin Acts. In Acts 1 Jesus tells His disciples that the good news about Him should be proclaimed to the whole world. He tells them to preach in "Jerusalem, Judea, Samaria and to the remotest parts of the earth."

The Gospel of John / Book of Acts	Week 18 Chapter paraphrase verses to memorize
☐ Day 86: John 18	Judas betrays Jesus
☐ Day 87: John 19	Jesus is crucified for our sins
☐ Day 88: John 20	Jesus is raised from the dead
☐ Day 89: John 21	Jesus appears to His disciples as the risen Savior!
☐ Day 90: Acts 1	Jesus ascends to heaven

*Review these each day and listen to the songs!

Key verse:

"Then He said to Thomas, 'Reach here with your finger, and see My hands; and reach here your hand and put it into My side; and do not be unbelieving, but believing.' Thomas answered and said to Him, 'My Lord and my God!'"
John 20:28

Did you know?

Church history tells us that Thomas was so persuaded of the resurrection he left Jerusalem and eventually ended up preaching the gospel all the way in India! Thomas was killed there while preaching his faith to the lost.

Prayer for the week:

Dear Father, thank You for the story of Thomas doubting the resurrection. I thank You that Jesus showed up and demonstrated to Thomas that He really was raised from the dead. Help me to not doubt but to trust in You fully this week!

The Book of Acts

Acts 2-6

Week 19

Weekly reading overview:

In Acts Chapter 2 God fills His church with His Holy Spirit. Peter stands up and preaches a sermon about the coming of the Spirit prophesied in the book of Joel. Three thousand people are saved that day! In Acts 3 Peter heals the lame man at the gate in Solomon's temple. This miracle creates quite a stir. Because of their continued preaching about Jesus, Peter and John are arrested by the Jewish authorities and told to stop preaching in Jesus' name. Peter and John say they cannot help but speak about the things they have seen and heard. Acts Chapter 5 tells the creepy story of Ananias and his wife Saphira. Just wait...In Acts 6, the disciples, overworked with all of the church's needs, elect several men who are full of the Holy Spirit to help minister to the church.

The Book of Acts	Week 19 Chapter paraphrase verses to memorize
☐ Day 91: Acts 2	The Holy Spirit descends on the apostles
☐ Day 92: Acts 3	Peter heals the lame man
☐ Day 93: Acts 4	Peter and John are arrested
☐ Day 94: Acts 5	The Holy Spirit is God
☐ Day 95: Acts 6	The first deacons are chosen

Review these each day and listen to the songs!

Key verse:

"And there is salvation in no one else; for there is no other name under heaven that has been given among men by which we must be saved."
Acts 4:12

Did you know?

Christians worship the One triune God of the Bible. We worship God the Father, God the Son, and God the Holy Spirit. One God in three persons. Don't think of the Father, Son, and Holy Spirit as 1+1+1=3. Think of God in higher math terms. Think of Him as 1x1x1=1. Each person is distinct, yet there is only one God.

Prayer for the week:

Dear Father, I thank You for the boldness of Peter and John in their preaching. Help me to be faithful to talk about the Gospel to those around me. Help me to never be afraid or ashamed of the message that saves.

The Book of Acts

Acts 7-11

Week 20

Weekly reading overview:

Acts 7 starts with the story of Stephen. Stephen was one of the deacons chosen in Chapter 6. He preaches an incredible sermon to the religious leaders demonstrating that Jesus is the fulfillment of all the Old Testament promises to Abraham. The people become so angry they... Well, you will see. In Acts Chapter 8 we meet Saul. He is a bad dude...but God is going to change him. In Acts 9 we see God get a hold of Saul. Jesus reveals Himself to Saul on the road to Damascus and changes his heart. In Acts 10 we meet Cornelius who is employed by the Roman army. God uses Peter to lead him to Christ. In Acts 11 Peter goes to Jerusalem.

The Book of Acts	Week 20 Chapter paraphrase verses to memorize
☐ Day 96: Acts 7	Stephen preaches the Gospel and gets stoned
☐ Day 97: Acts 8	Saul persecutes the church and the eunuch gets saved
☐ Day 98: Acts 9	Saul meets God on the road to Damascus
☐ Day 99: Acts 10	Cornelius gets saved
☐ Day 100: Acts 11	Peter goes to Jerusalem

Review these each day and listen to the songs!

Key verse:

"As he was traveling, it happened that he was approaching Damascus, and suddenly a light from heaven flashed around him; and he fell to the ground and heard a voice saying to him, 'Saul, Saul, why are you persecuting Me?' And he said, 'Who are You, Lord?' And He said, 'I am Jesus whom you are persecuting...'"
Acts 9:3-5

Did you know?

Saul is at the stoning of Stephen. Many have even claimed that Saul was responsible for it. In Acts 14 Saul, who begins going by the name of Paul, gets some of his own medicine. You will see next week what I mean.

Prayer for the week:

Dear Father, help me to have strength if persecution for following You ever comes to me. Help me to be strong like Stephen and stand up for truth. Lord, thank You for changing the heart of Saul on the road to Damascus!

The Book of Acts

Acts 12-16

Week 21

Weekly reading overview:

This week's reading is full of exciting stories about the early church. Acts 12 tells an amazing story of Peter's rescue from a prison cell. Chapter 13 tells the story of Paul's first missionary journey. Saul begins to use his Roman name, Paul, from this point on probably because he becomes the "Apostle to the Gentiles." Paul still preaches to Jews but mainly concentrates on preaching to the rest of the nations. Chapter 14 tells the story of Paul getting the same treatment as Stephen. Does he survive? Chapter 15 tells the story of an early church council meeting that included many of the apostles. It also talks about Paul's his second missionary journey. Pay attention to the drama with Mark and Barnabas. In Chapter 16 Paul has a vision telling him about the need to preach in Macedonia. The first city he visits there is Philippi. May God bless your reading this week!

The Book of Acts	Week 21 Chapter paraphrase verses to memorize
☐ Day 101: Acts 12	Peter is arrested, and the angel sets him free
☐ Day 102: Acts 13	Paul goes on his first missionary journey
☐ Day 103: Acts 14	Paul gets stoned for preaching the Gospel
☐ Day 104: Acts 15	Paul goes on his second missionary journey
☐ Day 105: Acts 16	Paul has a vision and preaches in Macedonia

Review these each day and listen to the songs!

Key verse:

"When the jailer awoke and saw the prison doors opened, he drew his sword and was about to kill himself, supposing that the prisoners had escaped. But Paul cried out with a loud voice, saying, 'Do not harm yourself, for we are all here!' And he called for lights and rushed in, and trembling with fear he fell down before Paul and Silas, and after he brought them out, he said, 'Sirs, what must I do to be saved?' They said, 'Believe in the Lord Jesus, and you will be saved, you and your household.'"
Acts 16:27-31

Did you know?

Acts 13:13 says that John Mark left Paul and Barnabas during the first missionary journey. We are never told why. When John Mark wants to go on the second missionary journey, Paul says no. Even though Paul seemed upset about John Mark, later he would say of John Mark, "Pick up Mark and bring him with you, for he is useful to me for service." (II Timothy 4:11)

Prayer for the week:

Dear Father, thank You for these great stories this week. Thank You for the endurance of the disciples. I pray that this week I will stay faithful to You in everything.

The Book of Acts

Acts 17-21

Week 22

Weekly reading overview:

Athens was filled with idol worship. The Athenians worshiped many false gods. They even set aside a place for an "unknown god" because they didn't want to offend one they may not have known. In Acts 17 Paul tells them about the TRUE GOD that they don't know. In Chapter 18 we see Paul's third missionary journey. In Chapter 19 we see some incredible miracles done in the city of Ephesus. In Chapter 20 Paul tells the churches that he is headed back to Jerusalem after his ministry among them is completed. In Chapter 21 the apostle Paul is accused of taking a Gentile into an area on top of the temple mount that is forbidden for Gentiles. It leads to some big trouble. Just wait!

The Book of Acts	Week 22 Chapter paraphrase verses to memorize
☐ Day 106: Acts 17	Paul preaches on Mars Hill
☐ Day 107: Acts 18	Paul goes on his third missionary journey
☐ Day 108: Acts 19	Paul preaches and does miracles in Ephesus
☐ Day 109: Acts 20	Paul warns the church about evil men
☐ Day 110: Acts 21	Paul is arrested in Jerusalem

Review these each day and listen to the songs!

"Therefore having overlooked the times of ignorance, God is now declaring to men that all people everywhere should repent, because He has fixed a day in which He will judge the world in righteousness through a Man whom He has appointed, having furnished proof to all men by raising Him from the dead."
Acts 17:30-31

This scripture clearly proves that Jesus is God. "Be on guard for yourselves and for all the flock, among which the Holy Spirit has made you overseers, to shepherd the church of God which He purchased with His own blood." (Acts 20:28) God purchased the church with His blood!

Dear Father, thank You for the boldness of Paul in the Bible. Thank You for using him to share the love of Jesus with those who didn't know You. Help me to do the same today.

Week 23

Weekly reading overview:

Paul was arrested during your last reading because he was accused of taking Trophimus who was a Gentile into the temple. In Chapter 22, Paul tries to defend himself, but that doesn't work out very well as you will see! In Chapter 23 Paul is moved to Caesarea because of a plot by several men to ambush and kill him. In Chapter 24 Paul preaches to Felix and tells him the story of how he came to faith in the gospel. Paul does the same with Festus and finally King Agrippa in Chapter 26. Agrippa is almost persuaded to become a Christian! In these chapters the authorities decided to send Paul back to Jerusalem to stand trial before the Jews. Paul doesn't want to return to Jerusalem because several men have pledged to kill him there. He has no choice but to appeal his case. When a Roman citizen appealed, he could appear before the highest Roman King called the Caesar. Paul appeals and is headed to Rome to appear before Caesar.

The Book of Acts	Week 23 Chapter paraphrase verses to memorize
☐ Day 111: Acts 22	Paul defends himself before the Jewish nation
☐ Day 112: Acts 23	Paul is moved to Caesarea
☐ Day 113: Acts 24	Paul preaches to Felix
☐ Day 114: Acts 25	Paul preaches to Festus
☐ Day 115: Acts 26	Paul preaches to Agrippa

Review these each day and listen to the songs!

Key verse:

"So, having obtained help from God, I stand to this day testifying both to small and great, stating nothing but what the Prophets and Moses said was going to take place; that the Christ was to suffer, and that by reason of His resurrection from the dead He would be the first to proclaim light both to the Jewish people and to the Gentiles."
Acts 26:22-23

Did you know?

Paul was a tent-maker by trade (Acts 18:3). The place where he was born, in Tarsus of Cilicia, was famous for making tents. The hair of mountain goats in that region was used for the making of the tents.

Prayer for the week:

Dear Father, thank You so much for the boldness of Paul to share the Gospel with the men of authority in these readings. I pray that this week I will share my faith with those around me who need to hear of Your great love for mankind.

The Books of Acts / Romans

Acts 27-28 + Romans 1-3

Week 24

Weekly reading overview:

The end of Acts details the account of Paul leaving Caesarea and heading toward Rome to stand trial before Nero the Caesar. It is amazing that he and Luke even survive the trip! Acts 28 ends with Paul awaiting his trial. This week you will begin reading an incredible letter that Paul wrote to the Roman church. In Romans 1 Paul begins by condemning the sins of the Nations (known as the Gentiles). In Chapter 2 Paul shifts his focus to the sins of his own people the Jews. In Chapter 3 Paul demonstrates that the scriptures teach all mankind is under a curse because of sin. There is no one who is good. Not even one! He does this to make sure everyone clearly understands that without Christ they deserve Hell. Only being in Christ can save a person!

The Books of Acts / Romans	Week 24 Chapter paraphrase verses to memorize
☐ Day 116: Acts 27	Paul is sent to Rome
☐ Day 117: Acts 28	Paul preaches boldly to the Romans
☐ Day 118: Romans 1	The just shall live by faith
☐ Day 119: Romans 2	The Law condemns all men
☐ Day 120: Romans 3	Everyone sins and needs the grace of God

Review these each day and listen to the songs!

 Key verse:

"For all have sinned and fall short of the glory of God, being justified as a gift by His grace through the redemption which is in Christ Jesus..."
Romans 3:23-24

 **Did you know?**

When Martin Luther read Romans 1:17 in the 16th century he realized that he couldn't do enough good works to please God. All He had to do was accept the free-gift of salvation through Christ by faith. When he began to preach about it, this preaching led to a period of history known as the Reformation.

 **Prayer for the week:**

Dear Father, I thank You so much that all I have to do is trust in the finished work of Christ in my place to receive salvation. I trust that You raised Him from the dead, and I ask You today to help me live a life pleasing to You.

Week 25

Weekly reading overview:

Romans 4 starts with the story of Abraham. Paul says that Abraham was right with God because of his faith in God, not because of any works he had done. Romans 5 tells us that our faith justifies us before God. In other words, our trust that Jesus took our place with his death and let us use His righteousness gives us a right standing before God. Romans 6 tells us that since we have given our lives to Jesus we should walk like He walked. Christ set us free from our old ways of serving ourselves. When He gives us His Spirit to live in us, we are changed from the inside out. Romans 7 teaches that before people come to Christ, they are trapped by the sin of their nature. Romans 8 teaches that when someone comes to true faith in the gospel, he is no longer enslaved to the old way of life, but has been set free to serve Jesus with a whole heart.

The Book of Romans	Week 25 Chapter paraphrase verses to memorize
☐ Day 121: Romans 4	Abraham believed God, and it was credited to him as righteousness
☐ Day 122: Romans 5	If we have been justified by faith we have peace with God
☐ Day 123: Romans 6	Be dead to sin and alive to God
☐ Day 124: Romans 7	The lost are in bondage to sin and death
☐ Day 125: Romans 8	Christ set the Christian free from sin and death

Review these each day and listen to the songs!

Key verse:

"For I am convinced that neither death, nor life, nor angels, nor principalities, nor things present, nor things to come, nor powers, nor height, nor depth, nor any other created thing, will be able to separate us from the love of God, which is in Christ Jesus our Lord."
Romans 8:38-39

Did you know?

A lot of Jews who professed to be followers of Christ in the first century were claiming that if someone was a Christian he must also do works of the Law. Paul argues in Romans 4 that Abraham was righteous before he did any work of Law simply by his faith in God.

Prayer for the week:

Dear Father, I pray that You will help me to never put trust in myself for salvation. Help me to have faith in You like Abraham. I trust You for eternal life, not anything I can do.

The Book of Romans — Romans 9-13

Week 26

Weekly reading overview:

Romans 9 retells the story of Jacob and Esau, that before they were ever born God had a plan for each of their lives. He has one for you as well! Chapter 10 tells us that we cannot justify ourselves before God. The Law was like a yoke hung around our necks that was too heavy for us to carry. We could never keep God's Laws perfectly. However, Jesus did *(Mt. 5:17)*. Romans 11 tells us that God desires both Jews and Gentiles to know and have a relationship with Him. Chapter 12 talks about spiritual gifts God gives to the church and how we should each use our gift to bless others in the church. Chapter 13 is all about honoring governmental authorities and loving our neighbors as ourselves.

The Book of Romans	Week 26 Chapter paraphrase verses to memorize
☐ Day 126: Romans 9	God controls the future of all men
☐ Day 127: Romans 10	Christ broke the yoke of the Law
☐ Day 128: Romans 11	God desires that all know him
☐ Day 129: Romans 12	Use your gifts to serve God and others
☐ Day 130: Romans 13	Love your neighbor as yourself

*Review these each day and listen to the songs!

 Key verse:

"Therefore I urge you, brethren, by the mercies of God, to present your bodies a living and holy sacrifice, acceptable to God, which is your spiritual service of worship. And do not be conformed to this world, but be transformed by the renewing of your mind, so that you may prove what the will of God is, that which is good and acceptable and perfect."
Romans 12:1-2

 **Did you know?**

YOU ARE EXACTLY HALF-WAY THROUGH THE NEW TESTAMENT! GREAT JOB! FINISH STRONG!

 **Prayer for the week:**

Dear Father, I trust Your plan for my life. I thank You that you promise to give me a spiritual gift when I believe in You. Please make clear to me what my giftings are so that I might serve You better.

You are exactly half-way through the New Testament! GREAT job! Finish STRONG!

Take a break and have some fun! Complete the activity review on the next page.

Can you match the paraphrase to the book and chapter?

[Draw a line from the blue to the correct paraphrase in yellow]

| God desires that all know him | Jesus is crucified for our sins | Jesus teaches about the greatest commandment | Jesus tells the parable of the Good Samaritan |

Luke 10 Matthew 22 John 19 Romans 11

Can you fill in the missing words to this key verse?

"And there is _____ in no one else; for there is no other _____ under _____ that has been given among men by which we must be _____."

_____ 4:___

The Books of Romans / I Corinthians

Romans 14-16 + I Corinthians 1-2

Week 27

Weekly reading overview:

Romans 14 is a great chapter where Paul encourages believers to put the need of their neighbor above their own. In Chapter 15 Paul encourages Christians from all different backgrounds to accept each other because Christ has accepted them. He also tells the Roman Christians that he plans to come to them on his way to Spain. Romans 16 is Paul's final goodbye to each of the churches in Rome. I Corinthians begins this week! In Chapter 1 the Apostle Paul tells the church to stop dividing over silly things. Each of the Corinthians were picking a preacher they liked and fighting about who was the best one. Paul says this is foolish. He also reminds them that God uses weak things like the cross of Christ to confound wise people. In Chapter 2 Paul tells believers to listen to the Spirit of God and not fall into the trap of living only for this life.

The Books of Romans / I Corinthians	Week 27 Chapter paraphrase verses to memorize
☐ Day 131: Romans 14	Build one another up in Christ
☐ Day 132: Romans 15	Accept one another just as Christ accepted you
☐ Day 133: Romans 16	Be wise in what is good and innocent in what is evil
☐ Day 134: I Corinthians 1	God uses weak things to confound the wise
☐ Day 135: I Corinthians 2	Have the Spirit of God not the spirit of the world

Review these each day and listen to the songs!

Key verse:

"Therefore, accept one another, just as Christ also accepted us to the glory of God."
Romans 15:7

Did you know?

Baptism cannot save a person. Only the Gospel can do that. Paul makes this clear in I Corinthians 1:17 when he says, "For Christ did not send me to baptize, but to preach the gospel, not in cleverness of speech, so that the cross of Christ would not be made void."

Prayer for the week:

"Dear Father, help me to accept people who are different from me. Help me to never look down on someone because they are from a different culture."

The Book of I Corinthians

I Corinthians 3-7

📅 Week 28

Weekly reading overview:

Chapter 3 teaches us that Christians are now the temple of God. Christians do not need to go to the Jewish temple to offer sacrifices to God. Jesus put an end to sacrifice (Heb. 10:12). We are holy because of Christ's work in us; therefore, we are the new temple. In Chapter 4, Paul talks about the hardship he and other disciples are going through for the cause of Christ. He continues to serve faithfully even though he has been hungry, thirsty, and without good clothing. In Chapter 5, Paul speaks to the Corinthians about a bad situation they have allowed to go on in the church. He tells them to discipline this man for his sin. Chapter 6 reminds Christians that Christ died for them, and because of this, we should seek to glorify God with everything we have. Chapter 7 is a great chapter for Christians to read carefully when considering marriage. Paul lays out some excellent guidelines for Christians to follow.

The Book of I Corinthians	Week 28 Chapter paraphrase verses to memorize
☐ Day 136: I Corinthians 3	Christians are the temple of God
☐ Day 137: I Corinthians 4	Serve God through every trial
☐ Day 138: I Corinthians 5	Discipline the wicked in the church
☐ Day 139: I Corinthians 6	You were bought with a price, glorify God with your bodies
☐ Day 140: I Corinthians 7	God makes the rules about marriage

Review these each day and listen to the songs!

 **Key verse:**

"Or do you not know that your body is a temple of the Holy Spirit who is in you, whom you have from God, and that you are not your own? For you have been bought with a price: therefore glorify God in your body."
I Corinthians 6:19-20

 **Did you know?**

Most people don't realize that many times Paul and the other disciples were hungry, thirsty, poorly clothed, roughly treated, and even homeless! *(I Cor. 4:11)*. Many Christians around the world are going through these same things today. Don't forget them in your prayers!

 **Prayer for the week:**

Dear Father, I pray for all Christians who are living in difficult circumstances around the world. I pray for Your protective hand around them and that You will help them to be faithful to Your calling on their lives.

The Book of I Corinthians

I Corinthians 8-12

 Week 29

Weekly reading overview:

In this week's reading, Paul encourages Christians not just to live for their own needs, but always to remember how their decisions will impact other believers. In fact, we should be willing to give up some of our rights to make sure that those around us are good in their relationship with Jesus. Chapter 9 encourages believers to use their freedom as Christians to bring glory to God. Whatever we do, it should all be for the glory of the Lord. Chapter 10 reminds us that no matter what our situation, God is with us and helps us in our time of temptation. Chapter 11 encourages Christians to imitate Jesus as they walk in the Spirit. In Chapter 12 Paul talks about how God blesses the church with different spiritual gifts and the importance of every gift. When all the gifts work together in harmony, it brings great glory to the Lord.

The Book of I Corinthians	Week 29 Chapter paraphrase verses to memorize
☐ Day 141: I Corinthians 8	Don't cause your brother to stumble
☐ Day 142: I Corinthians 9	Use your liberty for God's glory
☐ Day 143: I Corinthians 10	God is with you in temptation
☐ Day 144: I Corinthians 11	Be imitators of Christ
☐ Day 145: I Corinthians 12	Every spiritual gift comes from God

Review these each day and listen to the songs!

Key verse:

"No temptation has overtaken you but such as is common to man; and God is faithful, who will not allow you to be tempted beyond what you are able, but with the temptation will provide the way of escape also, so that you will be able to endure it."
I Corinthians 10:13

Did you know?

I Corinthians 9 makes clear that pastors in your churches should be paid by the congregation for their service to the church. I Corinthians 9:14 says, "So also the Lord directed those who proclaim the gospel to get their living from the gospel."

Prayer for the week:

Dear Father, help me to remember that all gifts that You give to the church are important in Your sight. Please reveal to me the gifts that You have given me and help me to use them for Your glory.

The Books of I Corinthians / II Corinthians

I Corinthians 13-16 + II Corinthians 1

Week 30

Weekly reading overview:

This week's reading starts with Chapter 13, known as "the love Chapter." Paul encourages Christians to remember the true meaning of love toward God and one another. In Chapter 14, Paul tells the Corinthians that worship services should be orderly. People should not be out of control at a worship service, but should serve God with reverence. Chapter 15 is the longest chapter in all of Paul's New Testament writing. This chapter talks about what it will be like when Christ returns. Paul speaks at length about God giving each Christian a new spiritual body that will last forever. All Christians who have died will receive a new body when the resurrection of the church occurs. If Jesus were to come back right now, all living Christians would receive a new body, one that will never wear out! Chapter 16 records Paul's closing words to the Corinthians. Paul's second letter to the Corinthians begins this week. Chapter 1 talks about the hardships and difficulties Paul faces as he continues to faithfully proclaim the gospel.

The Books of I / II Corinthians	Week 30 Chapter paraphrase verses to memorize
☐ Day 146: I Corinthians 13	Love is the most excellent way
☐ Day 147: I Corinthians 14	Worship should be orderly
☐ Day 148: I Corinthians 15	God promises a spiritual body
☐ Day 149: I Corinthians 16	Stand firm in the faith, be men and women of courage
☐ Day 150: II Corinthians 1	Be faithful to God through hardships

Review these each day and listen to the songs!

Key verse:

"In a moment, in the twinkling of an eye, at the last trumpet; for the trumpet will sound, and the dead will be raised imperishable, and we will be changed."
I Corinthians 15:52

Did you know?

When Christ returns, He will come with the spirits of all Christians who have died in the past *(I Thess. 4:14)*. Their bodies will be raised and instantly their souls will be reunited with their bodies *(I Corinthians 15:52-53)*. Jesus also talked about this *(John 5:28-29)*.

Prayer for the week:

Dear Father, I thank You that Christians do not have to fear death. I thank You that the souls of Christians are with You right now and one day You will even raise their bodies from the dead to make them new again. I thank You for these amazing promises!

The Book of II Corinthians

II Corinthians 2-6

Week 31

Weekly reading overview:

Paul starts this week by talking about Christians being led in triumph. During a Roman triumph, the General led his prisoners of war through the streets of Rome while the people cheered. Christians were persecuted and harshly treated in the first century. Being led in triumph was not a good thing. It means the Christians were being persecuted. In Chapter 2 Paul tells us that Christ has fulfilled all of God's laws in our place. As believers we carry the message of the gospel inside our earthly bodies. The gospel is like a treasure hidden inside of us that is released when we tell others about Jesus. Chapter 5 tells us that the moment a Christian dies, he is instantly in the presence of the Lord. Do you remember what Jesus said to the thief on the cross? "Today, you will be with me in paradise."*(Lk. 23:43)* Chapter 6 warns us about relationships with unbelievers. A Christian is to be a light to the unbelieving world but should be careful not to become entangled with unbelievers. The Bible says "bad company corrupts good morals." *(I Cor. 15:33)*.

The Book of II Corinthians	Week 31 Chapter paraphrase verses to memorize
☐ Day 151: II Corinthians 2	Christians are the fragrance of Christ
☐ Day 152: II Corinthians 3	Jesus lifted the veil of the Law
☐ Day 153: II Corinthians 4	We have God's treasure in earthen vessels
☐ Day 154: II Corinthians 5	To be absent from the body is to be present with the Lord
☐ Day 155: II Corinthians 6	Do not be bound together with unbelievers

Review these each day and listen to the songs!

Key verse:

"He made Him who knew no sin to be sin on our behalf, so that we might become the righteousness of God in Him."
II Corinthians 5:21

Did you know?

Paul is the author of II Corinthians. His name means "little." He was probably a small man and not a good speaker (II Corinthians 11:6). He was so boring at times that a man fell asleep while he was preaching, fell out a window, and died (Acts 20:9). Paul states that the Corinthians say of him, "his personal presence is unimpressive and his speech contemptible." (II Corinthians 10:10). Yet God used Paul to write the majority of the New Testament. God can use anybody!

Prayer for the week:

Dear Father, thank You that I have the treasure of the Gospel inside my life. Please help me to tell others about what You have done in me so that they might have that same treasure.

The Book of II Corinthians

II Corinthians 7-11

Week 32

Weekly reading overview:

At times Paul had to be harsh with the Corinthians because of their sin. He tells them in Chapter 7 that godly sorrow produces repentance. Repentance is truly changing your ways. Do you remember when Judas was sorry for betraying Jesus and threw the money back to the religious leaders? He was sorry, but didn't change his ways. True, godly sorrow produces change! In Chapter 8 and 9 Paul encourages the Corinthians to give an offering that he is taking to help people having a difficult time in Jerusalem. He encourages them to give generously and from a pure heart. Chapter 10 reminds us how important it is for us to be on guard with our thoughts. We should make all of our thoughts obey Jesus. Chapter 11 warns us that even though something looks good, it may be from the devil. He disguises himself as an angel of light. Sin sometimes looks appealing, and you want to do it. After you do the sin it leaves you empty because Satan is a deceiver.

The Book of II Corinthians	Week 32 Chapter paraphrase verses to memorize
☐ Day 156: II Corinthians 7	Godly sorrow produces repentance
☐ Day 157: II Corinthians 8	Give to others generously
☐ Day 158: II Corinthians 9	God loves a cheerful giver
☐ Day 159: II Corinthians 10	Take every thought captive to the obedience of Christ
☐ Day 160: II Corinthians 11	Satan disguises himself as an angel of light

Review these each day and listen to the songs!

Key verse:

"For you know the grace of our Lord Jesus Christ, that though He was rich, yet for your sake He became poor, so that you through His poverty might become rich."
II Corinthians 8:9

Did you know?

Bible scholars have long thought Ezekiel Chapter 28 speaks about Satan before his fall. It talks about his beauty before his sin against God. Isaiah 14 is another passage that many believe talks about Satan. The name used for him there is Lucifer, which means "light bearer." This could be why Paul says he appears as an angel of light.

Prayer for the week:

Dear Father, I pray that You will always help me to be generous to others in need. I also pray, Lord, that You will help me to not be deceived by those who will try to lead me away from You.

The Books of II Corinthians / Galatians

II Corinthians 12-13 + Galatians 1-3

Week 33

Weekly reading overview:

This week you will finish II Corinthians and begin Galatians. In Chapter 12 Paul talks about the difficulties of ministry. He says God has left him a "thorn in the flesh." We don't know exactly what Paul is talking about, but apparently this weakness, whatever it was, helped him to rely more on God. In Chapter 13 Paul tells the Corinthians to test their lives. Are they bearing fruit? Are they truly Christians? In Galatians 1 Paul tells the Galatians that the gospel is to be guarded carefully. In fact, he says that if an angel from heaven preaches to the Galatians a different gospel than they received from Paul, that the false angel is to be cursed by God! In Chapter 2 he reminds the Galatian believers they cannot be good enough on their own to get to heaven. They must trust in Christ's sacrifice for their sins alone for their salvation. In Chapter 3 Paul tells Christians that the laws of God brought death but that Jesus' keeping of the law in our place and sacrifice for our sins has made us right with God.

The Books of II Corinthians / Galatians		Week 33 Chapter paraphrase verses to memorize
☐ Day 161: II Corinthians 12	God's power is perfected in weakness	
☐ Day 162: II Corinthians 13	Test yourselves to see if you are in the faith	
☐ Day 163: Galatians 1	If anyone distorts the Gospel he is accursed	
☐ Day 164: Galatians 2	By the works of the Law no flesh will be justified	
☐ Day 165: Galatians 3	Christ redeemed us from the curse of the Law	

Review these each day and listen to the songs!

Key verse:

"I have been crucified with Christ; and it is no longer I who live, but Christ lives in me; and the life which I now live in the flesh I live by faith in the Son of God, who loved me and gave Himself up for me."
Galatians 2:20

Did you know?

There were a group of people in Galatia called "Judaizers." These people were telling the Galatian church that they should believe in Jesus, but they should also observe the Laws of God including a practice called "circumcision." Paul says that these people are wrong. Jesus' finished work alone is what makes a person right before God. Our good works will never earn us heaven or help us get into heaven.

Prayer for the week:

"Dear Father, thank You for the Gospel. Help me to be able to spot those who try to change Your truth. Thank You for saving me from the curse of the Law."

The Books of Galatians / Ephesians

Galatians 4-6 + Ephesians 1-2

Week 34

Weekly reading overview:

Trying to keep God's laws perfectly is impossible for us. You don't believe me? Try it for a couple of days, and you will feel like a slave! Jesus kept the laws perfectly for us. Because of this, when we have faith in His work, we become His sons and daughters. Galatians 5 tells us that a battle is being waged inside Christians. To follow God's will would be walking according to the Spirit. To sin would be walking in the flesh. Paul tells us to listen to the Holy Spirit and walk in the Spirit. Chapter 6 reminds us that anyone can fall into sin so when we correct someone, we should do it with a spirit of humility. We should even help that person carry the burden. Ephesians begins this week. It is an exciting book! Chapter 1 tells us that the blood of Christ is what saves us. Chapter 2 reminds us that we have done nothing to earn our salvation. Do not put trust in your own works of goodness. They can never get you into heaven. You must rely on the grace of God. Grace means that you don't earn your salvation. It is a free gift.

The Books of Galatians / Ephesians — Week 34 Chapter paraphrase verses to memorize

☐	Day 166: Galatians 4	We are no longer slaves but sons of God
☐	Day 167: Galatians 5	Walk by the Spirit, not by the flesh
☐	Day 168: Galatians 6	Bear one another's burdens
☐	Day 169: Ephesians 1	In Him we have redemption through his blood
☐	Day 170: Ephesians 2	It is by grace you have been saved through faith

Review these each day and listen to the songs!

Key verse:

"For by grace you have been saved through faith; and that not of yourselves, it is the gift of God; not as a result of works, so that no one may boast."
Ephesians 2:8-9

Did you know?

The city of Ephesus was famous for having one of the seven wonders of the ancient world, the Temple of Artemis. It was over 400 feet long with 127 columns each over 60 feet tall. A statue of Artemis in the back of the temple was so tall her head stuck out the top of the building! Look up an artist's reconstruction of it.

Prayer for the week:

Dear Father, help me to encourage those who fall into sin. Remind me that I am no better than them and could fall into the same trap. Help me to come along side of them and help them bear their burden.

The Books of Ephesians / Philippians

Ephesians 3-6 + Philippians 1

Week 35

Weekly reading overview:

A Gentile is a non-Jewish person. Paul reminds the Ephesians that Jesus' love is for the whole world, both Jew and Gentile. Anyone can come to Him through faith. Jesus gives the great commission to His disciples and tells them to preach the good news to the whole world (Acts 1:8). Have you ever heard someone try to say that words don't matter? Ephesians 4 tells us that words do matter and that the words of our mouths need to be God-glorifying. Chapter 5 reminds us to make the most of our time and be about building the church. Chapter 6 reminds us that Christians are engaged in a spiritual battle. Paul gives instructions on how to prepare for the battle in this important chapter. This week you will also begin a great letter Paul wrote to the Philippian believers while he was in prison awaiting trial before Caesar. He tells the believers that if he continues to live it will be for Jesus. If he dies, it will be gain because he will meet his savior in heaven!

The Books of Ephesians / Philippians — Week 35 Chapter paraphrase verses to memorize

☐	Day 171: Ephesians 3	The love of Christ is for Jews and Gentiles
☐	Day 172: Ephesians 4	Let no unwholesome word come out of your mouth
☐	Day 173: Ephesians 5	Walk as wise men and build the church of God
☐	Day 174: Ephesians 6	Put on the full armor of God
☐	Day 175: Philippians 1	For me to live is Christ and to die is gain

*Review these each day and listen to the songs!

Key verse:

"Children, obey your parents in the Lord, for this is right. Honor your father and mother (which is the first commandment with a promise), so that it may be well with you, and that you may live long on the earth."
Ephesians 6:1-3

 Did you know?

The President of the United States is always guarded by an elite special team called the Secret Service. This group of men and women will protect the president at all costs and even give their lives for the president. The King of Rome (called Caesar) also had an elite group that protected him called the Praetorian Guard. Paul says he had the opportunity to preach to them (Phil. 1:14) and we think some of them ended up as Christians! (Phil. 4:22)

 Prayer for the week:

Dear Father, I pray that You will guard all of the words that come out of my mouth. May they always be pleasing to You.

The Books of Philippians / Colossians

Philippians 2-4
+ Colossians 1-2

Week 36

Weekly reading overview:

Philippians 2:5-11 is a famous passage of scripture known as the "Song of Christ." It tells about the love God has for us and how He became a man and suffered in our place. In Chapter 3 Paul reminds the inhabitants of Philippi that this life is temporary and that they have an eternal home awaiting them in heaven. In Chapter 4 Paul tells the Philippians about some of his hardships and how he has learned to be content no matter what his circumstances are. He reminds the Philippians that God is the one who gives strength to the Christian in every circumstance. This week you get to begin another fantastic book called Colossians. In Chapter 1 we read that becoming a Christian allows us to move out of darkness and into light. Chapter 2 reminds us that we should not let our minds be taken captive by the lies of this world but instead remember that all truth comes from God. Paul also tells us that the fullness of God dwells in Jesus Christ.

The Books of Philippians / Colossians		Week 36 Chapter paraphrase verses to memorize
☐ Day 176:	Philippians 2	Have the same mind as Jesus Christ
☐ Day 177:	Philippians 3	Live as a citizen worthy of Christ
☐ Day 178:	Philippians 4	I can do all things through Christ who strengthens me
☐ Day 179:	Colossians 1	God rescued us from the domain of darkness
☐ Day 180:	Colossians 2	The fullness of God dwells in Christ

Review these each day and listen to the songs!

 Key verse:

"Finally, brethren, whatever is true, whatever is honorable, whatever is right, whatever is pure, whatever is lovely, whatever is of good repute, if there is any excellence and if anything worthy of praise, dwell on these things."
Philippians 4:8

 **Did you know?**

The city of Philippi was famous in the ancient world because of a huge civil war battle the nephew of Julius Caesar, Caesar Augustus, won there. After his victory, he made Philippi a retirement home for Roman soldiers. This could be why Paul tells the Philippians twice in his letter to remember where their citizenship comes from (Phil. 1:27; 3:20). They are citizens of heaven first, then citizens of Rome.

 **Prayer for the week:**

Dear Father, I pray that You will help me this week to remember that I am a citizen of heaven. Following You is a joy. Remind me that I belong to You and not to this world.

The Books of Colossians / I Thessalonians

Colossians 3-4 + I Thessalonians 1-3

Week 37

Weekly reading overview:

If you have given your life to Jesus and trusted in His death burial and resurrection in your behalf, the Bible teaches that you are saved. If you are truly saved God gives you His Holy Spirit to live within you. Over time, God begins to change you to become more like Jesus. Paul reminds the Colossian believers to seek Christ above all things. Again, Colossians 4 reminds us as we read in Ephesians last week, our words do matter. Our words need to be full of the grace and kindness of Jesus. This week we also begin the book of I Thessalonians. The church of Thessalonica was a very strong church located near Philippi. In Chapter 1 Paul reminds believers that the finished work of Jesus protects them from the day of judgment. Chapter 2 tells us that the gospel has been given to us by God, and we are to be careful to tell others about it in a right way. Chapter 3 reminds us that all Christians should have great love for one another. Don't forget what Jesus said about this, "By this all men will know that you are My disciples, if you have love for one another." *(John 13:35)*

The Books of Colossians / I Thessalonians	Week 37 Chapter paraphrase verses to memorize
☐ Day 181: Colossians 3	Since you've been raised up with Christ seek the things above
☐ Day 182: Colossians 4	Let all of your words be full of grace
☐ Day 183: I Thessalonians 1	Christ rescued us from the wrath to come
☐ Day 184: I Thessalonians 2	Christians have been entrusted with the Gospel
☐ Day 185: I Thessalonians 3	Abound in love for one another

Review these each day and listen to the songs!

Key verse:

"Therefore if you have been raised up with Christ, keep seeking the things above, where Christ is, seated at the right hand of God. Set your mind on the things above, not on the things that are on earth. For you have died and your life is hidden with Christ in God."
Colossians 3:1-3

Did you know?

The church of the Thessalonians was located in an area called Macedonia. These churches were very poor, but very generous in their giving toward the needs of others. Paul used the Macedonian churches as an example of what it means to be sacrificial in giving. *(II Corinthians 8:1-4)*. What a great example. Are you generous to others?

Prayer for the week:

Dear Father, thank You for your generosity toward me. Help me to be that way to all that I come into contact with. Thank You for Jesus!

The Books of I & II Thessalonians

I Thessalonians 4-5 + II Thessalonians 1-3

Week 38

Weekly reading overview:

Chapter 4 starts with a big word: sanctification, which means "God making sinners holy in heart and conduct."[1] God's will is for you to grow more like Him in your heart and in the way you act. Both chapters 4 and 5 talk about the return of Christ and urges Christians to always be ready! II Thessalonians begins by reminding the church that Christ will comfort Christians who are persecuted and that He will return to judge the world. Chapter 2 encourages us not to compromise our beliefs in the gospel but always to stand firm. Chapter 3 tells us that no matter how difficult things become to continue doing good. The word "weary" means to be tired. Don't grow weary in doing good!

The Books of I & II Thessalonians	Week 38 Chapter paraphrase verses to memorize
☐ Day 186 : I Thessalonians 4	Your sanctification is the will of God
☐ Day 187: I Thessalonians 5	Prepare for the coming of the Lord
☐ Day 188: II Thessalonians 1	Christ is returning to judge the world
☐ Day 189: II Thessalonians 2	Stand firm in the word of truth
☐ Day 190: II Thessalonians 3	Do not grow weary in doing good

Review these each day and listen to the songs!

Key verse:

"For the Lord Himself will descend from heaven with a shout, with the voice of the archangel and with the trumpet of God, and the dead in Christ will rise first. Then we who are alive and remain will be caught up together with them in the clouds to meet the Lord in the air, and so we shall always be with the Lord."
I Thessalonians 4:16-17

Did you know?

1 Thessalonians talks about dead Christians being resurrected at the second coming of Jesus. Many have wondered what the spiritual bodies of Christians will look like. We don't know too much about God's big plan, but the Apostle John says that we will be like Jesus' resurrected body. "We know that when He appears, we will be like Him, because we will see Him just as He is." *(I John 3:2)*

 Prayer for the week:

"Dear Father, I thank You that You conquered death and the grave. I thank You that the devil will not win, but in the end You will make us like Jesus and we will live forever with You."

[1] Thomas Ascol. Truth and Grace Memory Book 1. Founders Press 2017. Pg. 31

The Book of I Timothy

1 Timothy 1-5

Week 39

Weekly reading overview:

I Timothy is a great book and begins the section of the New Testament called the "pastoral letters." The other pastoral letters include II Timothy and Titus. Chapter 1 starts with Paul talking about how unworthy he is to receive the gospel. In truth, we all are, but God is a God of grace. In Chapter 2 Paul points out that Jesus is a mediator between us and God. A mediator comes between to people to bring peace. Because of Jesus' sacrifice in our place, He made us at peace with God the Father. In Chapter 3 we see God's Word explain what the character of leaders in the church should be like. In Chapter 4 Paul encourages Timothy; even though Timothy is young, he should be an example to others in the church. In Chapter 5 Paul talks about the importance of taking care of widows in the church.

The Book of I Timothy	Week 39 Chapter paraphrase verses to memorize
☐ Day 191: I Timothy 1	Christ Jesus came into the world to save sinners
☐ Day 192: I Timothy 2	There is one mediator between God and men, the man Christ Jesus
☐ Day 193: I Timothy 3	God makes the rules for church leaders
☐ Day 194: I Timothy 4	Let no one look down on your youthfulness
☐ Day 195: I Timothy 5	Take care of people in the church.

Review these each day and listen to the songs!

 Key verse:

 **Did you know?**

 **Prayer for the week:**

"By common confession, great is the mystery of godliness: He who was revealed in the flesh, was vindicated in the Spirit, seen by angels, proclaimed among the nations, believed on in the world, taken up in glory."
I Timothy 3:16

Many have argued that the Bible approves of slavery. The kind of slavery the Bible refers to is less like slavery and more like servanthood (*Exodus*). I Timothy 1:10 gives a list of sins including "kidnappers." The Greek word here literally means "men stealers." It refers to those who are a part of slave trading. The Bible is clear here that this is "contrary to sound teaching."

Dear Father, help me to be an example this week to others. Help me to realize the importance of walking with You and learning from You and Your Word daily.

The Books of I & II Timothy

I Timothy 6 + II Timothy 1-4

Week 40

Weekly reading overview:

Be careful with money! In Chapter 6 Paul reminds Timothy that loving money leads to all sorts of evil. II Timothy Chapter 1 tells us we should never be ashamed of Christ. No matter how difficult things get, we should remain faithful to our Lord. Chapter 2 tells us to be diligent in our pursuit of knowing God through His Word. We should constantly work at knowing and loving God more. Chapter 3 tells us that all scripture has come from God. He is the author and inspired men to record His Words. Paul encourages Timothy in Chapter 4 to always be ready to preach the gospel to those who need to hear it.

The Books of I & II Timothy	Week 40 Chapter paraphrase verses to memorize
☐ Day 196: I Timothy 6	The love of money is the root of all sorts of evil
☐ Day 197: II Timothy 1	Do not be ashamed of the testimony of Christ
☐ Day 198: II Timothy 2	Be diligent to present yourself approved to God
☐ Day 199: II Timothy 3	All scripture is inspired by God
☐ Day 200: II Timothy 4	Preach the Word; be ready in season and out of season

*Review these each day and listen to the songs!

Key verse:

"All Scripture is inspired by God and profitable for teaching, for reproof, for correction, for training in righteousness; so that the man of God may be adequate, equipped for every good work."
II Timothy 3:16-17

Did you know?

When our key verse says "All Scripture is inspired by God" it literally means "All Scripture is God-breathed." The Word of God comes directly from Him. He breathes His Word into being!

Prayer for the week:

Dear Father, I thank You that the Bible is God-breathed. I thank You that the Words are Yours and not merely those of men. I pray that You will help me to remember and know Your Word better today.

The Books of Titus / Philemon / Hebrews

Titus 1-3 + Philemon + Hebrews 1

Week 41

Weekly reading overview:

Titus is a little book with lots of great insight. Chapter 1 reminds us that the God we serve is a God of truth. He never misleads us. His Word is truth *(Jn. 17:17)*. In Titus 2 the Apostle Paul recounts the expectations for leaders in the church (much like I Timothy 3). He also encourages Titus and the churches who will hear the letter to be an example of good deeds to the outside world. Titus 3 provides great instruction on how Christians should treat each other with respect and kindness. This week you will also read the small letter of Philemon. In this book Onesimus has run away from his slave owner Philemon. Paul encourages Philemon to accept Onesimus when he returns and to remember that he is not only Philemon's servant but also a fellow brother in Christ. Hebrews 1 begins by telling us that Christ is greater than the angels.

The Books of Titus / Philemon / Hebrews	Week 41 Chapter paraphrase verses to memorize
☐ Day 201: Titus 1	God cannot lie
☐ Day 202: Titus 2	Show yourself to be an example of good deeds
☐ Day 203: Titus 3	Show consideration for all men
☐ Day 204: Philemon 1	Be obedient to authority
☐ Day 205: Hebrews 1	Jesus is the radiance of God's glory

Review these each day and listen to the songs!

 Key verse:

 **Did you know?**

 **Prayer for the week:**

"Looking for the blessed hope and the appearing of the glory of our great God and Savior, Christ Jesus, who gave Himself for us to redeem us from every lawless deed, and to purify for Himself a people for His own possession, zealous for good deeds."
Titus 2:13-14

Bible scholars aren't sure who wrote the book of Hebrews. However, the material contained in the book is solid, and the early church never doubted its truth, so Hebrews has always been a part of our New Testament. (Some think Barnabas wrote it.)

Dear Father, I thank You that Jesus put an end to the sacrificial system. I thank You that He was the perfect sacrifice for my sins. I thank You for Jesus' last words on the cross, "it is finished."

The Book of Hebrews

Hebrews 2-6

Week 42

Weekly reading overview:

Hebrews Chapter 2 starts by telling us not to drift away from following Christ but to hang in there and continue to trust God and His promises. Chapter 3 tells us that Christians should continue to encourage each other daily as they have fellowship with one another. Chapter 4 tells us that God's Word is living and active; it is never old or outdated. We will always continue to learn as we read and study God's Word. Chapter 5 reminds us that Jesus is better than the High Priests from Israel's past. The old High Priest repeatedly offered sacrifices each year, but Jesus offered His sacrifice for sins once and for all! Chapter 6 tells us that we should not be content to stay immature in the Christian faith. We should be striving to grow and become more like Christ.

The Book of Hebrews	Week 42 Chapter paraphrase verses to memorize
☐ Day 206: Hebrews 2	Jesus is the propitiation for our sins
☐ Day 207: Hebrews 3	Encourage one another every day
☐ Day 208: Hebrews 4	The Word of God is living and active
☐ Day 209: Hebrews 5	Jesus is the perfect High Priest
☐ Day 210: Hebrews 6	Christians should press on toward maturity

*Review these each day and listen to the songs!

Key verse:

"For the word of God is living and active and sharper than any two-edged sword, and piercing as far as the division of soul and spirit, of both joints and marrow, and able to judge the thoughts and intentions of the heart. And there is no creature hidden from His sight, but all things are open and laid bare to the eyes of Him with whom we have to do."
Hebrews 4:12-13

Did you know?

What does the word "propitiation" mean? It means "satisfaction." Jesus' sacrifice in our place satisfied the wrath of God that we deserved. God the Father is pleased with Jesus' death in our place. Jesus also lets us borrow His righteousness as our covering! (II Corinthians 5:21)

Prayer for the week:

Dear Father, help me to press on to maturity as a Christian. Help me to grow to be more like Jesus this week.

The Book of Hebrews

Hebrews 7-11

 Week 43

Weekly reading overview:

This week is full of great reading! Chapter 7 tells us that Jesus is the perfect priest. No priest in history compares to Him. Chapter 8 tells us that Jesus came to die in our place for our sins and to begin a new covenant with His people. Chapter 9 reminds us that sacrifice is necessary for our forgiveness, and Jesus is the perfect sacrifice. Chapter 10 continues by telling us that Jesus put an end to all sacrifice *(Heb. 10:12)*. He is the perfect sacrifice forever! Hebrews 11 recounts the faith of many great men and women from the past. Their examples for us are awesome!

The Book of Hebrews	Week 43 Chapter paraphrase verses to memorize
☐ Day 211: Hebrews 7	Jesus makes intercession for his people
☐ Day 212: Hebrews 8	Jesus is the mediator of a new covenant
☐ Day 213: Hebrews 9	Without the shedding of blood there is no forgiveness
☐ Day 214: Hebrews 10	The Law was a shadow of things to come
☐ Day 215: Hebrews 11	Without faith it is impossible to please God

Review these each day and listen to the songs!

 **Key verse:**

"And without faith it is impossible to please Him, for he who comes to God must believe that He is and that He is a rewarder of those who seek Him."
Hebrews 11:6

 **Did you know?**

Chapter 11 is known as the "faith chapter." This chapter tells the stories of many famous people from the past. Notice that all of them are described as having faith by what they do. The proof of their faith was their actions!

 **Prayer for the week:**

Dear Father, please help me to have faith like the godly heroes of the past. Please help me to always trust You even when it's difficult.

The Books of Hebrews / James

Hebrews 12-13
+ James 1-3

Week 44

Weekly reading overview:

Hebrews 12 tells us we are surrounded by those in heaven who have died before us and are rooting us on. As we run the race of the Christian life, we must keep our eyes fixed on the goal, Jesus! Chapter 13 tells us that God never changes. We can count on His character to be the same yesterday, today, and forever! This week we begin the book of James, written by the brother of Jesus. In Chapter 1 James encourages Christians not just to talk about following God, but to do it. Chapter 2 tells us that true biblical faith looks a certain way. God's people bear fruit in their lives. In Chapter 3, James warns that not everyone should teach the Word of God. Anyone teaching God's Word will be judged strictly. The Word of God is not to be trifled with.

The Books of Hebrews / James	Week 44 Chapter paraphrase verses to memorize
☐ Day 216: Hebrews 12	Fix your eyes on Jesus, the author and finisher of our faith
☐ Day 217: Hebrews 13	Jesus Christ is the same yesterday, today, and forever
☐ Day 218: James 1	Prove yourselves doers of the Word
☐ Day 219: James 2	Faith without works is dead
☐ Day 220: James 3	Teachers will incur a stricter judgment

Review these each day and listen to the songs!

 **Key verse:**

"*But prove yourselves doers of the word, and not merely hearers who delude themselves.*"
James 1:22

 **Did you know?**

James the brother of Jesus was known as James the Just. He was famous for being a very righteous man. He was the leader of the church in Jerusalem and made some very important decisions for the early church (Acts 15).

 **Prayer for the week:**

Dear Father, help me to not be distracted by the things of the world but to remain focused on You and Your glory. I pray that You will help me to live out my faith in the Gospel that people may see Your glory.

The Books of James / I Peter

James 4-5 + I Peter 1-3

Week 45

Weekly reading overview:

James 4 tells us that friendship with the world is hostility toward God. This doesn't mean you can't have friends who are not believers. It means you shouldn't love things of the world that pull you away from following Christ. James 5 tells us that God listens to the prayers of a righteous man. Take it from James who was a prayer warrior! I Peter was written by the famous disciple of Jesus named Peter. Chapter 1 tells us that God is holy. If we are His children, we should work hard to be like Him. In Chapter 2 Peter encourages us to remember that we have freedom in Christ, but that freedom is not an excuse for us to sin. We are called to a higher standard as Christians and should work hard at being holy. Chapter 3 encourages us always to be ready to give an answer to those who have questions about Jesus.

The Books of James / I Peter	Week 45 Chapter paraphrase verses to memorize
☐ Day 221: James 4	Friendship with the world is hostility toward God
☐ Day 222: James 5	The prayer of a righteous man accomplishes much
☐ Day 223: I Peter 1	Be holy because God is holy
☐ Day 224: I Peter 2	Do not use your freedom as a covering for evil
☐ Day 225: I Peter 3	Sanctify Christ as Lord of your heart

*Review these each day and listen to the songs!

Key verse:

"But sanctify Christ as Lord in your hearts, always being ready to make a defense to everyone who asks you to give an account for the hope that is in you, yet with gentleness and reverence..."
I Peter 3:15

Did you know?

James the brother of Jesus is famous for his prayer life. Church history says that he spent so much time on his knees praying that his knees had calloused over. His nickname was Camel knees!

Prayer for the week:

Dear Father, please make me a person of prayer like James. I pray that the desire to be faithful in prayer will be formed in me by Your Holy Spirit.

The Books of I & II Peter

I Peter 4-5 + II Peter 1-3

Week 46

Weekly reading overview:

It is important for Christians to exercise hospitality with one another. This is critical because Jesus said the world would know us by the love we have for one another *(John 13:35)*. I Peter 5 tells us that God is opposed to anyone who is prideful. When we come to God, we must come in humility, recognizing that we have nothing to give Him. Jesus gives us everything! II Peter 1 tells us that God is the one who gave us scripture by inspiring holy men to record His Word. Chapter 3 tells us that when Christ returns it will be like a thief in the night. Jesus told us in Acts 1 that it wasn't for men to know the time of His return. The important thing for us to remember is that we should be ready to meet Jesus at any time!

The Books of I & II Peter	Week 46 Chapter paraphrase verses to memorize
☐ Day 226: I Peter 4	Be hospitable to one another without complaint
☐ Day 227: I Peter 5	God is opposed to the proud but gives grace to the humble
☐ Day 228: II Peter 1	No prophecy was ever made by an act of the human will
☐ Day 229: II Peter 2	The Lord knows how to rescue the godly from temptation
☐ Day 230: II Peter 3	The day of the Lord will come like a thief in the night

*Review these each day and listen to the songs!

Key verse:

"*For no prophecy was ever made by an act of human will, but men moved by the Holy Spirit spoke from God.*"
II Peter 1:21

Did you know?

In our key verse it says that men "were moved by the Holy Spirit" when they wrote down the scriptures. This same phrase was used at the time to refer to boats at sea being blown by the wind.

Prayer for the week:

Dear Father, help me to love the body of Christ like I should. Help me to show hospitality to Your children and never complain. I thank You that Jesus loved me sacrificially.

The Book of I John

I John 1-5

Week 47

Weekly reading overview:

This week you will be reading the excellent book 1 John, written by John the disciple of Jesus. Chapter 1 tells us that God is light and in Him there is no darkness. His character is pure and holy. He is trustworthy and true. Chapter 2 tells us to remember that we were made for more than this world. We should love God above all things! Chapter 3 tells us not just to talk about the faith we have, but to live it out. Chapter 4 warns us to be careful and not believe just anyone who says he is speaking on behalf of God. We should test everyone's words by God's word. Chapter 5 tells us that if we love God we should obey God. Jesus says, "If you love Me, you will keep My commandments." *(John 14:15)*

The Book of I John	Week 47 Chapter paraphrase verses to memorize
☐ Day 231: I John 1	God is light and in Him there is no darkness at all
☐ Day 232: I John 2	Do not love the world nor the things in the world
☐ Day 233: I John 3	Let us love others in deed and in truth
☐ Day 234: I John 4	Do not believe every spirit but test the spirits
☐ Day 235: I John 5	This is the love of God: that we keep His commandments

Review these each day and listen to the songs!

Key verse:

"Do not love the world nor the things in the world. If anyone loves the world, the love of the Father is not in him. For all that is in the world, the lust of the flesh and the lust of the eyes and the boastful pride of life, is not from the Father, but is from the world."
I John 2:15

Did you know?

The apostle John who wrote the Gospel of John and I, II, and III John is the only disciple to not be killed for his faith.

Prayer for the week:

"Dear Father, I thank You for being light! I pray that You will help me to not hide my light under a basket but let it shine bright so that all may see You in me!"

The Books of II & III John / Jude / Revelation

II & III John + Jude + Revelation 1-2

Week 48

Weekly reading overview:

II John tells us once again that we should remain in the teachings of Christ. When we are unashamed of His teachings, we show the world we have the Father and the Son in our lives. III John encourages disciples of Jesus to walk in truth. God has great joy when we obey no matter what our circumstances (Remember the faith chapter? Hebrews 11). The small book of Jude tells believers they should contend for the faith. This means standing up against error and telling others the truth of God's Word. This week you begin the final book of the New Testament! Revelation will be tough to understand, but hang in there, you are almost finished! Chapter 1 tells us Jesus is the Alpha (the first letter in the Greek alphabet) and the Omega (the last letter in the Greek alphabet). This means that Jesus is the beginning and the end. He is God! *(John 1)*. Chapter 2 begins a section of letters to the different churches in Asia for which Revelation was originally written.

The Books of II & III John / Jude / Revelation	Week 48 Chapter paraphrase verses to memorize
☐ Day 236: II John	One who abides in the teaching has the Father and the Son
☐ Day 237: III John	I have no greater joy than to know that my children walk in truth
☐ Day 238: Jude	Contend earnestly for the faith
☐ Day 239: Revelation 1	Jesus is the Alpha and Omega
☐ Day 240: Revelation 2	God speaks to Ephesus, Smyrna, Pergamum and Thyatira

*Review these each day and listen to the songs!

Key verse:

"Beloved, while I was making every effort to write you about our common salvation, I felt the necessity to write to you appealing that you contend earnestly for the faith which was once for all handed down to the saints."
Jude 3

Did you know?

The Devil is a powerful being. Notice that when Michael the Archangel was in a dispute with him, he didn't rebuke the Devil himself but said, "the Lord rebuke you." (Jude 1:9)

Prayer for the week:

Dear Father, I thank you for allowing me to share about Jesus. Help me to be ready to defend the truth of the gospel with kindness and humility toward others.

The Book of Revelation

Revelation 3-7

Week 49

Weekly reading overview:

Revelation 3 finishes John's words to the different churches in Asia. He points out the sins they are committing and their need to turn from them. Chapter 4 is a beautiful description of the heavenly throne that stresses the holiness of God. The word "holy" means to be "set apart." God is not like us. He is holy and set apart from His creation. In Chapter 5 we see all of creation worshiping the Lamb of God (Jesus). People from every tribe, tongue, and nation worship Jesus together in heaven. Chapter 6 turns toward judgment, revealing four different horseman. The four judgments are carried by four riders on horses of different colors — white, red, black, and ashen. Chapter 7 reminds us that salvation comes from God through Christ!

The Book of Revelation	Week 49 Chapter paraphrase verses to memorize
☐ Day 241: Revelation 3	God speaks to Sardis, Philadelphia, and Laodicea
☐ Day 242: Revelation 4	Holy, Holy, Holy is the Lord God
☐ Day 243: Revelation 5	Jesus will be worshipped by all creatures
☐ Day 244: Revelation 6	The four horsemen and judgments are revealed
☐ Day 245: Revelation 7	Salvation to our God who sits on the throne and to the Lamb

*Review these each day and listen to the songs!

Key verse:

"Worthy is the Lamb that was slain to receive power and riches and wisdom and might and honor and glory and blessing." **Revelation 5:12**

Did you know?

At the end of Revelation 5, we see all of creation bowing down before Christ. A reminder of what Paul said in Philippians 2:10-11 "so that at the name of Jesus every knee will bow, of those who are in heaven and on earth and under the earth, 11 and that every tongue will confess that Jesus Christ is Lord, to the glory of God the Father."

Prayer for the week:

Dear Father, I thank you for giving salvation to your people. I am excited for the day to come when all of creation bows down before you.

The Book of Revelation Revelation 8-12

 Week 50

Weekly reading overview:

In the next couple of chapters, we see judgments poured out upon the earth. Bible scholars disagree on many of the symbols in the book of Revelation and also on when the events described will take place. In Chapter 10 John is told to take God's Word into himself and prophecy to the nations. Chapter 11 talks about two witnesses who will appear in the end times. Some have said the two witnesses would be Enoch and Elijah. Others have wondered if they are the Old and New Testament. No one really knows for sure. Chapter 12 tells the story of Satan being cast out from the presence of God.

The Book of Revelation	Week 50 Chapter paraphrase verses to memorize
☐ Day 246: Revelation 8	The seventh seal is opened
☐ Day 247: Revelation 9	God's judgment is poured out
☐ Day 248: Revelation 10	John is told to prophesy to the nations
☐ Day 249: Revelation 11	The two witnesses appear
☐ Day 250: Revelation 12	Satan is cast out from the presence of God

*Review these each day and listen to the songs!

 **Key verse:**

"The kingdom of the world has become the kingdom of our Lord and of His Christ; and He will reign forever and ever."
Revelation 11:15

 **Did you know?**

Satan is not a name. It is actually an adjective meaning "accuser." We don't know his name. The words devil, and lucifer are the same, just adjectives. We do know that he is a fallen angel (Ez. 28; Rev. 12).

 **Prayer for the week:**

Dear Father, help me to remember that in the end, Satan will lose the final battle. You will reign victorious over all evil forever."

The Book of Revelation

Revelation 13-17

Week 51

Weekly reading overview:

You only have two weeks to go! Chapter 13 talks about the mark of the beast. Many Bible scholars have argued about the identify of the beast. Some have said it was Nero, the Emperor of Rome. Others have said it will be an end- time figure. One thing is for sure, we must remain on the alert! Chapter 14 contains a beautiful section about those who are set apart as God's children (14:1-5). Chapter 15 talks about the nations coming to worship God. These passages demonstrate that the Great Commission will one day be completely fulfilled (Mt. 24:14). Chapter 16 talks about the bowls of God's wrath, His fierce judgments upon the earth. Chapter 17 tells us that God's great enemy is destroyed by the power of the Lamb of God, Jesus.

The Book of Revelation	Week 51 Chapter paraphrase verses to memorize
☐ Day 251: Revelation 13	The beast gives his mark to the world
☐ Day 252: Revelation 14	God's people sing to him a new song
☐ Day 253: Revelation 15	Great and marvelous are your works, oh Lord God Almighty
☐ Day 254: Revelation 16	The six bowls of wrath appear
☐ Day 255: Revelation 17	Babylon the Great is defeated by the Lamb of God

Review these each day and listen to the songs!

 **Key verse:**

 **Did you know?**

 **Prayer for the week:**

"Great and marvelous are Your works, O Lord God, the Almighty; righteous and true are Your ways, King of the nations!"
Revelation 15:3b

A lot of people are afraid that in the last days they will receive the mark of the beast talked about in chapter 13. You don't need to be afraid, though. Christians have their own mark, given to them by God. (Revelation 14:1)

"Dear Father, I thank you that you know your children and have sealed and marked them for the day of salvation. Thank you God for following through on all of your promises."

The Book of Revelation

Revelation 18-22

 # Week 52: The last week!!!

Weekly reading overview:

THIS IS IT! DID YOU MAKE IT? Babylon the Great, mentioned in Chapter 18, is not the real Babylon from history. Babylon refers to any country or people opposed to God. In the end they will be defeated by God. In Chapter 19 we see Jesus returning as the King of Kings and Lord of Lords. What a day that will be when He returns! Chapter 20 tells us Satan will be judged by God. Chapter 21 speaks beautifully about the end when the heavens and the earth merge into a New Jerusalem. This will be God's new creation where every tear is wiped away from every eye. Chapter 22 ends perfectly by reminding us to be ready. Jesus says "I am coming quickly!" **Are you ready?**

The Book of Revelation	Week 52 Chapter paraphrase verses to memorize
☐ Day 256: Revelation 18	Babylon is judged and comes to an end
☐ Day 257: Revelation 19	Christ returns as King of Kings and Lord of Lords
☐ Day 258: Revelation 20	Satan is bound, freed, and judged
☐ Day 259: Revelation 21	The New Jerusalem is revealed for believers
☐ Day 260: Revelation 22	Jesus tells his people, "Yes, I am coming quickly!"

*Review these each day and listen to the songs!

"Then I saw a new heaven and a new earth; for the first heaven and the first earth passed away, and there is no longer any sea. And I saw the holy city, new Jerusalem, coming down out of heaven from God, made ready as a bride adorned for her husband."
Revelation 21:1-2

The study of the last times is called eschatology. It isn't important when Jesus will come back. It is important that He comes back, and He has promised us that He will! (Acts 9:1-11, Rev. 22:20)

"Dear Father, I so look forward to your return. I pray that I would be ready at all times and that when you come again I will be found a faithful disciple of Jesus."

Way to go!!! You finished the entire New Testament.

260 › **52** › **27**

Days
Chapters
Paraphrases

Weeks
Key verses
Fun facts
Prayers

Books

Hope you enjoyed your time doing *New Testament 260*. The next page is just for fun!

Draw/write something new you learned:

What is your favorite paraphrase?

I am thankful to God for:

1. _____
2. _____
3. _____

The Gospel of _____ is my favorite.

FUN FACT! Which fact did you find most fun?

My favorite key verse is _____.

My favorite book of the New Testament is _____.

Made in the USA
Monee, IL
12 January 2020